"We are on a journey—a journey of change and transformation.
Everything we need to know lies within us.
May the words that follow lead you to your inner guidance
and make your path a smoother and more joyful one.
May they be words that heal."

## WORDS THAT HEAL

"A creative and heartfelt book of meditations."

—Ralph Blum,
author of *The Books of Runes*

"A fine, gentle book."

—New Age retailer

"Just the thing to lift your spirits and fill you with inspiration
. . . full and evocative."

—*New Realities*

"An inspiring and uplifting guide, I recommend *Words That Heal* to anyone who is on the path to recovery."

—Casey C., Alanon

"*Words That Heal* is the most helpful book on affirmations I have ever had the pleasure to read. I am grateful to Douglas Bloch for making this resource available to us all."

—Barry Knowles,
Unity minister

"Ancient wisdom translated into modern terms . . . the best book on affirmations I have seen."

—Lucia Capacchione
author of *The Power of the Other Hand*

# BANTAM NEW AGE BOOKS

This important imprint includes books in a variety of fields and disciplines and deals with the search for meaning, growth and change.
Ask your bookseller for the books you have missed.

*Affirmations and Meditations
for Daily Living*

# WORDS
# THAT
# HEAL

## Douglas Bloch

**BANTAM BOOKS**
NEW YORK · TORONTO · LONDON · SYDNEY · AUCKLAND

This edition contains the complete text
of the original hardcover edition.
NOT ONE WORD HAS BEEN OMITTED.

WORDS THAT HEAL

A Bantam Book / published by arrangement with
the author

PRINTING HISTORY

Pallas Communications edition published 1988
Bantam edition / January 1990

**Library of Congress Cataloging-in-Publication Data**

Bloch, Douglas, 1949–
    Words that heal : affirmations and meditations for daily living /
Douglas Bloch.
        p.    cm.
    ISBN 0-553-34809-4
    1. Meditations.   2. Spiritual life.   I. Title.
BL624.B55   1990
291.4'3—dc20                                                89-6960
                                                                CIP

Published simultaneously in the United States and Canada

PRINTED IN THE UNITED STATES OF AMERICA

OPM      0  9  8  7  6  5  4  3  2  1

"Goodbye," said the fox.
"And now here is my secret, a very simple secret:
It is only with the heart that one can see rightly;.
what is essential is invisible to the eye."

"What is essential is invisible to the eye," the little prince repeated,
so that he would be sure to remember.

Antoine de Saint-Exupéry

*This one, at last,
is for my mother and father.*

# ACKNOWLEDGMENTS

The act of creation is one of the most challenging of all human endeavors. Fortunately, many individuals generously donated their time and support to the creation of *Words That Heal*. Although the original inspiration came one November morning in 1980, the book first took form in 1982 during my stay at Findhorn, a spiritual community in Northern Scotland. In particular, I was influenced by the works of Eileen Caddy, who demonstrated how to listen to the still small voice within.

Five years later, on Christmas Eve of 1987, I was guided to return to the project. At this critical juncture the support of my friends and editors, Kay David and Ann Garrett, proved invaluable. During the next three months they served as spiritual midwives, guiding and directing the birth of *Words That Heal*. As the birth process continued, the following people provided additional editorial input: Mary Allen, Brian Bergeron, Cathy Brenner, James Cloutier, Pat Dempsey, Jim Estes, Leanne Langford, Fran Mathis, Lucy Oxenhandler, Marika Plesko, Betty Sikking, Marzenda Stiles, Carol Schaeffer, Diana Stone, Robert Wasner, and Julie Weiss. In addition, Casey Chaney offered the perspective of the 12–step recovery process to the work. The written text was greatly enhanced by the book design work of L. Graffix.

Finally, thanks as always go to my wife, Joan, and to my parents for their continued support of my writing and teaching.

---

The meditations and affirmations in *Words That Heal* provide healing for specific psychological and spiritual challenges that we all face. Below are listed some of those conditions along with the passages that offer direct guidance on how to heal and transform them.

To heal **loss** or **grief,** turn to pg. 30, 58, 60, 70, 98, or 100.

To heal **anger** or **resentment,** turn to pg. 48, 54, 100, 102, or 112.

To heal **fear,** turn to pg. 42, 54, 82, 84, or 128.

To heal **helplessness** or **hopelessness,** turn to pg. 36, 40, 68, 90, or 108.

To heal **health** problems, turn to pg. 32, 64, 106, or 132.

To heal **uncertainty** or **anxiety** about the future, turn to pg. 32, 34, 62, 66, 72, or 96.

# CONTENTS

# CONTENTS

# CONTENTS

# WORDS
# THAT
# HEAL

# How to Use This Book

*Words That Heal* is a book of spiritual guidance that is designed to:

Help you to use the creative power of thought to shape your own reality;

Provide you with daily inspiration that will raise your spirits and enhance the quality of your life;

Get in touch with your inner knowing.

For many centuries, humanity depended upon institutions and doctrines to lead it to the experience of God-consciousness. As we approach the dawn of a new age, we are learning to rely upon **our own intuition** to experience the divinity within.

The heart of *Words That Heal* consists of 52 passages or "teachings," each of which contains three parts:

1) A **Meditation**—a short passage that offers thoughts and reflections about a specific subject or life experience. Each meditation will speak to you in its own way, providing support, comfort, insight, and understanding.

2) **Affirmations**—positive thoughts and ideas that, when repeate, will help you to heal and transform your beliefs and attitudes. For those readers not familiar with affirmations, the text begins with an overview of what affirmations are and how to use them.

3) A **Quotation** that summarizes the essence of the teaching.

While it is possible to read the passages straight through as you would a novel, think of the book as a collection of individual stories, each of which tells its own tale and can be approached one at a time.

Refer to *Words That Heal* as you would any other inspirational work. You can consult with it on a regular basis or periodically, whenever you feel the need to go within and dwell in your "secret place of the most high."

We are on a journey—a journey of change and transformation. Everything we need to know lies within us.

May the words that follow lead you to your inner guidance and make your path a smoother and more joyful one.

May they be words that heal.

# Affirmations:
# The Power of Positive Speaking

*"My word that goes forth from My mouth*
*shall not return to Me void,*
*But it shall accomplish that which I please,*
*and it shall prosper in the thing for which I sent it."*
Isaiah 55:11

# The Power of Positive Speaking

"What you say is what you get." This simple statement demonstrates one of the most important tools of spiritual self-development—**Affirmations**. Let's briefly explore the nature of affirmations and how you can use them to shape your inner and outer reality.

An *Affirmation* is a positive thought or idea that you consciously focus on in order to produce a desired result. The affirmation is a simple yet powerful technique that can heal and transform your most deeply held beliefs.

## How Affirmations Work

Affirmations are based upon the following principles:
1) Your outer reality is a direct reflection of your predominant thoughts and beliefs.
2) Change your thoughts and you change your reality.
3) Your thoughts manifest through the written and spoken *word*.

A few years ago, I left a secure job to pursue my writing full time. Consequently, I was a bit anxious and apprehensive about how I would fare. To allay my fears, I created the following affirmation: *I have the ability to create support for myself in my life*.

Upon repeating these words to myself, silently and out loud, I experienced a calmness, confidence and decrease in my fear. The effect was subtle, but clearly noticeable. During the next few weeks, whenever I felt self-doubt or anxiety, I simply recited the affirmation and experienced a state of peace and serenity.

More than allaying my fears, I was reprogramming my subconscious mind to believe that I could succeed in my new work. This new belief led to corresponding behaviors which created the outcome I desired—a series of completed books.

That is the first level of how affirmations work—by making life a self-fulfilling prophecy. When boxing great Muhammad Ali first proclaimed "I AM THE GREATEST," he was a relatively unknown boxer named Cassius Clay. Ten years and thousands of repetitions later, he was hailed as the greatest fighter of all time. Ali had tapped into the power of the affirmation.

## When to Use Affirmations

Affirmations can be used whenever you wish to bring some good that you desire into your life. You can employ affirmations to achieve a **specific goal** or **outcome** in the outer world. "I have now found the perfect home," "I am enjoying a new job with a great company," and "The cells of my body radiate with health" are examples.

In addition, you can use affirmations to heal your inner world by focusing on a positive **attitude** or **belief.** Sample affirmations of this type are "I deserve love," "I now forgive my parents," and "I like myself."

A wonderful truth about affirmations is that an affirmation exists for *every* need. Whatever the situation, you can always speak the word for it.

## How to Create Healing Affirmations

Using affirmations to heal your life is a simple and enjoyable process. What follows is a method that I have found quite effective.

**Pick an area of your life that needs healing.**
The topic of your affirmation can involve a relationship, your health, work, finances, peace of mind, etc. For an example, let's choose the area of relationships. Perhaps you have been carrying around some old anger that you are now ready to release.

**Decide what you want to occur in that area of your life.**
Ask yourself, "What would it feel like if this part of my life were healed?" In our example, you probably want to let go of the anger and experience peace and forgiveness.

**Using the first person, formulate a concise statement that expresses the desired outcome.**
As you choose your words, keep in mind the following points:

1) Write your affirmation in the **present** tense, as if the experience were happening in *this* moment. The point of power is in the present. Thus, you would say *I am peaceful* instead of *I will become filled with peace*.

2) State it **positively**. When you say, *I am not angry*, the subconscious mind screens out the "not" and hears *angry*. If someone says to you, "Don't think of pink elephants," that exact image will immediately come to mind. To prevent this

7

from occurring, rephrase the affirmation to **directly** state what you want—e.g. *I now release my resentment*.

### Experience how it feels.

Once you have written your affirmation, say it to yourself a few times. When you have found a good affirmation, it will "click." It will feel right to you (ful*feel*ment brings fulfillment). If the affirmation doesn't quite work, you can fine tune it by altering one or two words. Thus, *I am experiencing peace* may work better if stated as *I am at peace* or *I am peace*.

### Repeat your affirmation each day.

Say it to yourself, say it out loud, or write it down. Repetition is the mother of learning. Consider the affirmation "Every day, in every way, I am getting better and better." Imagine filling your subconscious with these healing words day after day. Over time, your mental and emotional outlook would clearly improve.

When you repeat an affirmation, you impress its thought pattern on your mind, thereby transforming your previously held beliefs. The more you use your affirmation, the more rapid and powerful the healing will be. Soon its words will become a **living** presence in your awareness. Later, you will actually **become** the words. When you repeat the affirmation *I am peace*, you will **become** peace. When you say *I am love*, you **are** love.

### Be consistent.

It is essential to use your affirmation on a daily basis in order to benefit from the principle of spaced repetition. It takes time for new response patterns to be formed in the brain. You may also wish to set aside a specific time each day to focus on your affirmations such as upon awakening or before bedtime.

**Turn the final outcome over to a higher power.**

How many times have you thought you wanted something, only to realize later that having it would have been a major fiasco? Oftentimes, we affirm a certain want or desire when in fact the universe has something entirely different planned—something which is for our higher good. For this reason, I always conclude my affirmations with the following statement: *This or something better now manifests for me in totally satisfying and harmonious ways for the highest good of all concerned*. This way, I know that my will and the will of the universe are aligned.

## Techniques for Further Reinforcing Affirmations

Over the years, I have discovered a number of techniques that can reinforce your affirmations to make them more effective and powerful. Here are some of my favorites.

• **Use rhyme**. Words that rhyme seem to make a more powerful impression on the subconscious mind than blank verse. This principle is illustrated in the following story.

A man suffering from a physical illness received a healing affirmation from his minister. Soon his condition improved. "I guess that affirmation did the trick," the minister said when he heard the news. "Well, to tell you the truth," the man replied,

"I lost your affirmation the day after you gave it to me." "How then, did you heal yourself so quickly?" asked his puzzled friend. The man responded, "Since I couldn't remember your affirmation, I simply told myself, 'Oh, hell, I'm well.' "

Other rhyming affirmations include, "I play for pay," "I will Thy will" and "I feel fine when I'm on time." Experiment and create your own.

• **Sing** the affirmations to yourself once you have created a rhyme. The great Indian poet Tagore said, "God respects me when I pray, but he loves me when I sing."

• Place written copies of your affirmations on walls, the car dashboard, the refrigerator—anywhere that will make them **visible.** One woman sticks her affirmations to the bathroom mirror so that she sees them each morning and evening.

• Make a **cassette tape** of your affirmation using your own voice. You can play the tape as you fall asleep, upon awakening, or throughout the day.

• State your affirmation while you look at yourself **in the mirror.** This is a very powerful way of making contact with yourself.

• Incorporate **creative visualization** with your affirmations. See yourself experiencing the good that you desire in the present moment. Another application of this principle is to make a "treasure map"—a collage of pictures and words that creates a visual presentation of the good you are seeking.

Human beings have many different ways of perceiving. Thus, when you **say**, **see**, and **feel** your affirmation, your mental perceptions are powerfully combined to produce the optimum result.

• Give **thanks**, before or after your affirmation. This is based upon the principle, whatever you appreciate grows and expands. The affirmation "I am healthy and prosperous" becomes even more powerful when stated as "I give thanks for my health and prosperity." See if you can feel the difference.

• Create an **affirmation notebook** or **journal** in which you can record your affirmations and keep track of your progress over time.

These techniques have been tested over time by friends and students. I encourage you to incorporate them with your own affirmations.

## When Affirmations Don't "Work"

Although the principles behind affirmations are universally true, those who practice affirmations often experience mixed results. Here are some obstacles that can block the effectiveness of a good affirmation.

1) **The affirmation is not sufficiently repeated**. Remember, repetition is the mother of learning. Any new thought pattern must be repeated many times before it becomes a mental habit.

2) **The affirmation is not specific enough**. When a

friend at a workshop affirmed "I want more money," the trainer gave him twenty-five cents. The universe will respond in a similar manner unless you are specific and concrete about what you want.

3) **The affirmation lacks a strong feeling element**. A nonchalant approach will not work here. Your affirmation needs to be charged with feeling and intention.

4) **You don't really *believe* the affirmation to be true**. In other words, a part of you holds a thought that directly counters the affirmation. Almost everyone who uses affirmations faces this inner resistance. The more healing the affirmation, the stronger the resistance that comes up. As we will see in the pages that follow, learning to deal with this negative self-talk is essential if you wish to successfully use affirmations in your daily life.

## Using Affirmations to Uncover and Release Negative Beliefs

Assuming your affirmation is well stated, feels right, and is used consistently, the only thing standing between you and its realization is your own resistance. This resistance takes the form of those unconscious beliefs that are blocking expression of the desired state. Remember, your conscious mind is only the tip of your mental iceberg. The beliefs that create your inner and outer reality are located below the threshold of conscious awareness—known as the subconscious mind. It is here that your childhood memories, experiences and reality-creating beliefs are stored. The power of these subconscious attitudes is illustrated in the following example.

Suppose you want to work with Ali's affirmation "I am the greatest," in order to build your self-esteem. But perhaps your conditioning has led you to believe that you are incompetent. Thus, every time you tell yourself how great you are, your subconscious directly contradicts the statement with what it **knows** to be true. A typical dialogue is depicted below.

| Conscious Mind | Subconscious Mind |
| --- | --- |
| I am the greatest. | I'm afraid you're not. |
| I am the greatest. | In fact, you're a real loser. |
| I am the greatest. | You can't do anything right! |

The pattern is all too clear. Because your subconscious beliefs portray you as someone who can't get it together, your affirmations fall on deaf ears. Here is another example.

| Conscious Mind | Subconscious Mind |
| --- | --- |
| I deserve to be prosperous. | Money is the root of all evil. |
| I deserve to be prosperous. | Money will corrupt you. |
| I deserve to be prosperous. | You can't hold on to any money. |

What makes this process so insidious is that you may not even be aware that your subconscious mind is sabotaging

13

your efforts. Ignoring these subconscious beliefs is like painting over rust, or hacking away at weeds instead of pulling them up by the roots. The basic problem remains unchecked. Despite your best efforts, you remain stuck in old self-defeating patterns without knowing why.

Fortunately, there is a way out—**Make the subconscious conscious.** In other words, bring your most deeply held assumptions about life to the light of day where they can be experienced and released.

Using affirmations, the process is amazingly simple. Divide a sheet of paper into two columns. Label the left-hand column "**Affirmation**" and the right-hand column "**What Comes Up.**"

**Affirmation**                    **What Comes Up**

Then, after putting yourself in a relaxed and receptive state of mind, write your affirmation in the left-hand column. Afterwards, be still and notice what bubbles up from the subconscious mind. Then write the material down in the right-hand column, no matter how irrelevant it may appear. The process is similar to free association.

After you repeat this six or seven times, your right column will contain a list of the major negative beliefs and assumptions you hold regarding your affirmation. The process is analogous to rototilling the garden of your subconscious mind. In order to produce superior soil, you first clear away the debris, rocks, weeds and other unsuitable material. Then, when you add the fertilizer (affirmations), you will nurture only those plants (thoughts and beliefs) that you wish to grow.

Here is how it worked for Carol, whose goal was to open a fashion boutique specializing in used clothes.

| Affirmation | What Comes Up |
|---|---|
| I am successfully running my own business. | I can't do it. |
| I am successfully running my own business. | It's too much work. |
| I am successfully running my own business. | I need to be working at a regular 9-to-5 job. |
| I am successfully running my own business. | There's not enough money in it. |
| I am successfully running my own business. | You need something that provides more security. |
| I am successfully running my own business. | No one in your family is an entrepreneur. |

As you can see, Carol now has a clear knowledge of her core beliefs that tell her she "can't" own and run her own business. However, the process does not end here. If Carol continues to repeat the affirmation, the negatives will eventually exhaust themselves, to be replaced by positive thoughts and feelings that emanate from her Higher Self. For example:

| | |
|---|---|
| I am successfully running my own business. | I have excellent taste in clothing. |
| I am successfully running my own business. | I know other people who own their own businesses. |
| I am successfully running my own business. | If they can do it, so can I. |
| I am successfully running my own business. | If they can do it, I can too. |
| I am successfully running my own business. | With God, all things are possible. |
| I am successfully running my own business. | I know I can succeed. |

Now we're getting somewhere. Using the principle of thought substitution, Carol's negative beliefs are being replaced by positive attitudes that will draw to her the good that she desires.

## Dealing With Getting Stuck

As old habit patterns are particularly ingrained, the two column process may have to be repeated a number of times before your affirmation can be firmly established. The amount of time required will depend on the strength of the old belief, your desire to change, and how often you use your affirmation.

Most negative beliefs that appear in the right-hand column will eventually disappear on their own. If a particular belief continues to persist, you can reprogram your mental computer by asking yourself the following questions:
1. How did I obtain this belief? Who communicated it to me?
2. Is there any truth to it now?
3. Am I ready to release the belief?

When you are ready to release your old belief, do so by changing it into a new affirmation as demonstrated in the following sentence.

"I now release the belief that _____" (write down your old belief), "and I now replace it with _____"(write your new belief or affirmation).

Let's review the process using as an example Carol's negative belief "I need to be working at a nine-to-five job." The reprogramming might proceed as follows.
1. How did I obtain this belief? *My mother gave it to me.*
2. Is there any truth to it now? *Not at all.*
3. Am I ready to release the belief? *I am ready.*

I now release the belief that *"I need to be working at a nine-to-five job"* and replace it with the new belief *"I succeed by being self-employed."*

All healing consists of *awareness* and *choice*. Once you become aware of your limiting beliefs, you can choose to release those which are causing you pain and replace them with those which support you. Although the new beliefs may feel unfamiliar at first, over time they will become a part of you. If the old patterns continue to resist change, you may wish to seek out a therapist, counselor, priest, minister, rabbi, friend— anyone who can be a guide and assist you through the process of growth and transformation.

Another way to get support is through a support group. You may want to get together with other friends who are using affirmations to share your progress and give feedback. Or you can incorporate affirmations into a support group you already belong to.

## Using Affirmations to Transform Lifelong Challenges

In the course of a lifetime, each of us has one or more lifelong challenges to deal with. Much of our spiritual growth occurs through healing and transforming these core issues which emerge out of our core beliefs. Most of these beliefs were formed at a very early age (from birth to seven) when we learned concepts of **who we are** and **how the world works**. During this period, the discriminating, evaluating mind was not fully developed, and so whatever programming we received entered the subconscious mind unedited. Unfortunately, much of this programming was negative, given by people—usually parents, relatives, teachers, and in some cases our peers—who themselves were negatively programmed.

Once internalized, these beliefs become our own and begin to manifest in our lives. A friend whose parental message was "you always are losing things" developed the habit of misplacing objects. On the other hand, the mother of a four-year-old boy sat outside his bedroom each evening and repeated "You can do anything you want to do." Later on, he was able to perform many feats that his teachers and friends thought impossible. Now he uses affirmations with his own children.

It is also important to note that messages are communicated both verbally and nonverbally. Because children learn through modeling, they unconsciously absorb their parent's attitudes and beliefs.

Thought is magnetic. In life, we receive what we attract. And what we attract is determined by our most deeply held beliefs. What we believe to be the absolute truth, on both conscious *and* unconscious levels, is what we create in our lives. As adults, it is our responsibility to take inventory of these beliefs, keep the ones that are serving us, and release the ones that are detrimental.

How do you learn what your beliefs are? You can find out by completing the affirmation exercise and observing the statements in your right-hand column. They will give you a clear picture of your beliefs regarding that particular affirmation. A second method is to look at your life as an outer expression of your core beliefs. Thus, if you want to learn about your beliefs about money, look at your bank account; for your beliefs about relationships, observe the state of your marriage or your friendships; for your beliefs about health, look at the condition of your body, etc. If any of these areas is out of alignment, it is a good indication that you are holding a negative belief or attitude about that area. Since the root of these mental and emotional blockages resides in thought, affirmations are an excellent tool to change the ingrained patterns.

Take a moment and reflect upon a specific core belief in your life that you wish to **heal**. To identify one, it may help to think in terms of the following categories: Self-Esteem, Love and Relationships, Health, Work/Vocation, Prosperity, Creative Self-Expression, and Spiritual Development.

Once you have identified your issue, find an affirmation whose message contains a *resolution* of that challenge. Remember, whatever the situation, the perfect affirmation exists to heal it. The appendix offers a list of affirmations to choose from, or you can compose your own. For example, if your primary core issue is lack of **trust**, your affirmation might be, "I live in a safe and loving universe."

Write down your core issue and its healing affirmation in the space provided or on a separate piece of paper.

**My core issue** _____

**Affirmation that** _____
**will heal this challenge** _____

Now it is time to work with the affirmation in depth. Start by repeating it to yourself throughout the day. Write your affirmation down and post it in your home where you will be sure to see it on a regular basis. To clear away any negative conditioning, use the technique you learned earlier when you divided a sheet of paper into two columns and allowed those beliefs to surface and be released.

People often ask how long they should work with a particular affirmation. Use your affirmation until the good you are seeking is attained. Let's say you are affirming the purchase of a new home. After you buy it, the affirmation will have served its purpose. If you decide to move at a later date, you can always return to the affirmation.

Another common question is "How many affirmations should I use at a time?" To avoid scattering your energies, it is best to start out by focusing on one or two affirmations. As you become more skilled at the process, you can add more to your list. George Washington once said, "I remove my faults one at a time." Likewise, with affirmations it's best to release one negative belief at a time.

Be patient, persevering and persistent. Over time your personal affirmation will take on a life of its own and change your inner reality according to the words you have spoken. When you affirm, you are saying YES! to your universe.

I encourage you to work with affirmations. *Words That Heal* was written in order to teach how language can be used to heal and transform our lives. I can think of no better and simpler way to apply the creative power of thought than by using affirmations in your daily life.

# The Main Text

*"Great thoughts come from the heart."*
Chinese Proverb

# Using the Main Text

The following 52 "teachings" comprise the main text of *Words That Heal*. Each teaching contains three parts:

1) A **Meditation**—a short passage that offers thoughts and reflections about a specific subject or life experience. Each meditation will speak to you in its own way, providing support, comfort, insight, and understanding.

2) A Series of **Affirmations**—positive thoughts and ideas that when repeated will help you to transform your negative beliefs and attitudes. For those readers not familiar with affirmations, the previous chapter provides an overview of what they are and how to use them.

3) A **Quotation** that summarizes the essence of the teaching.

While it is possible to read the passages straight through as you would a novel, think of the book as a collection of individual teachings, each of which tells its own tale and can be approached one at a time.

### Selecting a Passage
When you are ready, pick a comfortable spot in your environment. If you make a habit of meditating, you can use your normal meditation area. Otherwise, find a space where you will not be disturbed for a while.

Next, choose your passage. People have found various ways of selecting the text. Here are a few ideas to consider:

1) Start with the first passage and read the rest in order. Since there are 52 in all, you can focus on one for each week of the year.

2) Look through the Table of Contents and choose a theme that best reflects an important issue you are now facing.

3) Open the book at random, and read what is in front of you.

The last method, called dowsing, is my favorite. I find that I invariably turn to the teaching that is just perfect for me at that point in time. Try it and see what happens!

Once you have selected your passage, you may want to repeat a simple prayer or invocation that will place you in a receptive frame of mind for the reading. One example is:

*As I enter this meditation, I affirm that the Divine presence fills my body, mind, heart and soul. From this place of higher knowing, I now receive whatever wisdom, guidance, or healing I need at this time.*

Now glance at the **meditation**, **affirmations**, and **quotation**. As they were designed to function as a whole unit, you can read them in order. Or perhaps one section may appeal to you more than the other. Let your intuition be your guide, drawing to you whatever words you need to receive.

Let your mind be open to the fruits of the spirit—thoughts of peace, comfort, serenity, and joy. You may also experience a sense of clarity, especially if you are using this process to receive guidance or direction on some point.

At any time, you may wish to write down your insights in a separate notebook or journal. If you are inspired to create your own affirmations, you can write them down in the space provided in this book or in your own notebook/journal.

## Responding To Negative Emotions

Sometimes, old thoughts and feelings may bubble up from your subconscious mind that represent unresolved, painful experiences from the past. If this occurs and you begin to feel some discomfort, allow yourself to experience your feelings as they arise. In most cases, they will diminish in intensity after a while. Experiencing and releasing old pain is part of the healing process.

If, however, any thoughts or emotions come up that are overly unpleasant, you may want to seek the aid of a friend, counselor or therapist who can help you to process these unresolved feelings. There are many such trained "guides" who offer the knowledge and experience to assist you on your transformational journey. An inspiring discussion on the role of psychotherapy as a tool for spiritual development is contained in M. Scott Peck's *The Road Less Traveled*.

## The Higher Power

The meditations that follow speak of a higher power. We refer to this intelligence by many names: "God," "Higher Power," "Spirit," "Light," "Cosmic Consciousness," "Christ Consciousness," "The Divine," "The Is," "The Universe," "The Force," "Infinite Intelligence," "I Am," or "Higher Self."

As there are many ways to describe this cosmic energy, feel free to think in those terms that are most comfortable to you. If you were brought up in a traditional setting, the word "God" may feel just fine. If, on the other hand, you rebelled against this type of upbringing or were reared in a secular home, you may be more comfortable with a neutral term such as Higher Self or Infinite Intelligence.

The important thing to remember is that these terms depict an essence that is beyond any words, thoughts, or concepts you may have.

The universe is intelligent, loving and communicative. In the following pages, you will have the opportunity to directly experience that part of your "self" that can guide, direct and heal your life. Open yourself to this inner knowing. It is waiting to serve you.

# ONE

# When one door closes, another door opens

When one door closes, another door opens. Have patience, perseverance and persistence.

There comes a time along the spiritual journey when something we cherish must come to an end. Perhaps a meaningful relationship is terminated. Perhaps some opportunity we sought suddenly becomes unavailable. Whatever the circumstances, we feel shut out from a good that we desired.

When this occurs, do not despair, for the Infinite has not forgotten you. You have experienced loss for one reason and one reason only—so that you may receive an even **greater good.**

Nature abhors a vacuum. What is true in the physical world has its parallel in the spiritual world. You can't release something without gaining something in return. The universe longs to fill your void, replacing sadness with joy, loss with gain, death with rebirth.

What then is your task when a door is closed before you? First, release your attachment to the way it **was**, or the way you **wished** it to be. Your Higher Self has prepared a far greater gift for you. Then affirm to yourself, *"When one door closes another door opens. I expectantly look forward to the good that awaits me."*

Be patient, for it will come in the twinkling of an eye.

## *Affirmations*

1. I release the past and eagerly look toward the good that awaits me.

2. I release my prior expectations and allow a benevolent universe to support me.

3. I have faith that I am being guided to my next step.

4. Although I grieve for what I lost, I know that a greater good will follow.

5. A new door in my life stands open before me.

6. Your own _____

_____

**Words To Consider**
*"They that sow in tears shall reap in joy."*
Psalm 126.5

# TWO

# Let go and let God

Our spiritual growth requires that we face many challenges and trials along the path. Although we must meet these tests face on, we do not have to face them alone. We have the reassurance of one who said, "Come to Me all you who labor and are heavy laden ... for My yoke is easy and My burden is light."

Let go and let God. When you call upon the **source** of all things and *let it work* **through** *you*, you will tap into the very power that created the universe. Think how much more you can accomplish with this force as your ally.

As you cast your burdens over to that Higher Power within you, obstacles that seemed insurmountable are overcome. The road ahead becomes clear. With the Infinite as your partner, there is nothing you can't accomplish. With God, all things are possible.

Letting go and letting God requires faith. There is only one way to develop this trust—by stepping out and experiencing the results. In order for the universe to support you, you must give it a chance to do so.

Now is the time to release your fear and move forward. Take that first step into a new way of life. Let go and let God, and experience that loving support which is your birthright.

# *Affirmations*

1. I allow higher wisdom to direct and guide my way.

2. When I let go and let God, everything works out.

3. Not my will, but Thy will be done.

4. I surrender to my Higher Self, asking what "it" wants me to do.

5. The universe nurtures and supports me at all times, and in all places.

6. Your own _____
_____

**Words To Consider**
*"What the caterpillar calls the end of the world,
the master calls a butterfly."*
Richard Bach

# THREE

# One day at a time

One of the most important lessons of the spiritual life is that of trust. We must learn to trust ourselves and trust the universe. There is no better way of developing this faith than by living one day at a time, fully immersed in the present and attentive to the inner voice.

There was a man who was experiencing a great deal of pain. At first, he focused on getting through each week. Then, as the pressure increased, he strove simply to survive each day. Finally, as his test came to a climax, he held on for each hour. That is how he lived, sixty minutes at a time. Each hour that passed represented a glorious victory, until he ascended out of the darkness and into the light.

Whether you are experiencing a period of calm or a time of transition, live one day at a time. Focus solely on the moment, taking no thought for tomorrow. If what you are doing now feels right, trust the process and continue with it. And when the time comes that you are called upon to make a change, listen to your inner voice; the next message will come at the exact moment that you need it.

As you begin to live in the present moment, you will experience a subtle but profound change. Worrying about the future will cease. A deep peace will enfold you, a peace that says, "All is well. There is nothing to fear. Everything is unfolding according to plan, and you are being guided each step along the way."

# *Affirmations*

1. I focus fully on the present moment; the future takes care of itself.

2. Focusing on the present heals my fear of the unknown.

3. I am in full communication with my inner guidance.

4. Whatever I am ready for is ready for me.

5. Living one day at a time brings me peace, joy and serenity.

6. Your own _____

_____

**Words To Consider**
*"Life must be lived forwards,*
*but can only be understood backwards."*
Kierkegaard

# FOUR

# I choose the world in which I live

Of all the gifts you have been given, your ability to **choose** is the most precious. Through the use of your free will, you are called to participate with the Infinite in the act of creation. You are called to be a co-creator with God.

Being a creator enables you to experience the **consequences** of your choices. This is the primary way to grow and to evolve toward a higher awareness. When you make choices that are in alignment with your highest good and that of others, you experience pleasurable consequences. If, however, you go against the grain of your Divine nature, you experience painful results. Through this process of trial and error, you gradually learn to choose only the good.

Look around at the condition of your world (your health, finances, relationships, vocation) and you will see the results of the choices you have made. If you are dissatisfied with these conditions, you have the power to change them. There is no one else who can assume that responsibility for you.

The most important aspect of exercising choice is the ability to **choose how to respond** to a given situation. Perhaps you have experienced a personal loss, an unexpected illness, or some other apparent setback. Choose now to bless the situation, and see it as contributing to your highest good. Search out its meaning, and you will discover a spiritual teaching that will more than compensate for your present pain.

"I choose the world in which I live." What a joy, and what a responsibility! Accept your divine inheritance and use your free will to create heaven on earth.

## *Affirmations*

1. I am the master of my fate, I am the captain of my soul.

2. I use my creative power to bring the best into my life.

3. As the writer and director of my own movie, I can change the script whenever I wish.

4. I assume responsibility for me.

5. I choose to see the best in every situation.

6. Your own _____

_____

**Words To Consider**
*"It matters not how strait the gate,
how charged with punishment the scroll.
I am the master of my fate,
I am the captain of my soul."*
William Ernest Henley

# FIVE

# Empty yourself and receive

Consider the following story. A Japanese monk went to visit his venerable teacher to receive some words of inspiration. Before they sat down, the Master offered his pupil some tea. As the Master poured, the pupil's cup filled and began to overflow onto the floor. "Why are you continuing to pour?" cried the student. "Can't you see that the tea is spilling all over?" The teacher replied, "Your mind is like that cup. How can I pour in anything new unless you first empty it of its mental contents?"

You, too, are like this cup. To receive the awareness of the Divine, you must strive to empty your mind and your heart of all your wordly thoughts and prejudices. As you begin to empty yourself totally, you will make room for that Higher Power to enter. Like spring waters rushing to replenish an empty lake, feelings of peace, joy, serenity, and love will fill the silence of your being.

"Be still and know that I am God," wrote the psalmist. Take a moment now to be silent. Quietly repeat to yourself, "I open my heart and mind to receive the presence of God." Then listen. In the stillness that follows, you will experience a fullness of spirit that is deeply healing.

# Affirmations

1. I make myself an empty vessel to receive the spirit of God.

2. I am ready, Lord, to receive Your spirit.

3. I can tap into my inner guidance at all times and in all places.

4. My inner voice communicates with me clearly and willingly.

5. In my stillness, I experience a deep and joyous peace.

6. Your own _____

_____

**Words To Consider**
*"Be still and know that I am God."*
Psalm 46:10

# SIX

# Don't give up five minutes before the miracle

The journey to higher awareness is not a direct flight. Challenges, struggles and tests confront the traveler along the way. Eventually, no matter who you are or how far you have come along the path, you must experience your "dark night of the soul."

If you are facing such a period, let these words console you:

**What Goes Down Must Come Up.**
There can be no death without rebirth.
Every ending is followed by a beginning.
The experience of hell is a precursor to the glory
of heaven.

The process of death and rebirth is universal. The legendary Phoenix bird was consumed in flames only to rise from its own ashes. Christ was crucified only to be resurrected. Your case is no exception.

When you are in pain, the feelings of despair may be so great that you feel you can no longer continue. Nevertheless, the prescription is simple: hang in there! Be patient. Soon you will find a way to rise out of your ashes and spread your wings like a soaring eagle. The joy that awaits you is far greater than the pain you are experiencing.

Don't give up five minutes before the miracle!

# Affirmations

1. What goes down must come up; I know this to be true in my life.

2 I am in the process of being reborn.

3. I can sense the light at the end of the tunnel.

4 I can feel the sun coming over the horizon.

5. I expect a miracle to occur at any moment.

6. Your own _____

_____

**Words To Consider**
*"Never are we nearer the Light
than when the darkness is deepest."*
Vivekananda

# SEVEN

# Alone I stand united

No matter how isolated you may feel at times, you are never truly alone for the presence of God dwells within you at all times. Whether you find yourself on an ocean beach or in the midst of a modern city, at a social gathering or sitting alone, you can call upon that indwelling presence. Once you have joined with that inner divinity, you will never feel separate again.

In the Divine presence, you live, move and have your being. When you are truly immersed in this presence, you feel whole, complete, connected and loved. Nowhere is this feeling more important than in times of loss on the material plane. Perhaps something or someone upon whom you depended has left. Maybe a hope, wish, or dream has been dashed. Yet, in the midst of the emptiness, one relationship remains. One friend beckons from within you. One bridge will never be dismantled.

You are like the man who while walking along the beach, saw two sets of footprints, one his own and one belonging to God. During his lowest and saddest times, however, he saw only one set. Thinking he had been abandoned, the man cried out and asked why he had been deserted. The Infinite replied, "I would never leave you. When you saw only one set of footprints, it was then that I carried you."

Close your eyes and experience that connectedness. Feel the peace and serenity that come from drinking from a fountain whose waters will eternally quench your thirst.

Alone you stand united.

# *Affirmations*

1.  I am connected to the Infinite Intelligence of the universe.

2.  Wherever I am, God is.

3.  I experience the presence of God within me.

4.  I am one with Divine love.

5.  The universe nurtures me at all times and in all places.

6.  Your own _____
    _____

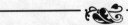

**Words To Consider**
*"Lo, I am with you always,*
*even unto the end of the world."*
Matthew 28:20

# EIGHT

# Seek God first

Oftentimes we think of our spiritual life as secondary to the concerns of the "real world"— work, money, family, relationships, health, etc. But, in reality, just the opposite holds true. When you make your spiritual life your first priority, then all other priorities fall into place. When you raise your consciousness to a higher awareness, you become a divine magnet that attracts all desired and needed things to you.

This principle is beautifully demonstrated by the story of Solomon. One night God appeared to Solomon in a dream and said, "What shall I give you?" Instead of requesting riches, fame, or power, Solomon asked for *"an understanding heart."* The Divine was so pleased by this request that it responded, "Behold, I have done according to your words; see, I have given you a wise and understanding heart ... and I have **also** given you what you have not asked: both riches and honor so that there shall not be anyone like you among the kings all your days."

Solomon asked for spiritual discernment and received both wisdom and material prosperity. He turned his heart to the inner kingdom and all else came to him. These same riches are available to you if you put your spiritual development first.

## *Affirmations*

1.  I put my spiritual life first.

2.  I commune with God first in the temple of silence; then health, prosperity, and wisdom are drawn to me.

3.  Union with God is my primary goal.

4.  I am one with Divine love.

5.  When I make God my highest priority, all other priorities fall into place.

6.  Your own _____

_____

**Words To Consider**
*"Seek ye first the kingdom of heaven,*
*and all these things shall be added unto you."*
Matthew 6:33

# NINE

# Giving is receiving

The law of giving flows from this truth: rather than being a fixed entity, the universe is a dynamic, flowing, moving stream of energy. When you give of yourself unconditionally, you create a temporary imbalance that must be corrected. Like the molecules of air rushing in to fill a vacuum, the universe strives to replace the good you have given out.

Often, the flow will come back from a totally unexpected source. For example, you may spend a day helping Anne move into her new home. Six months later when it is your turn to move, Anne may be unavailable to help you, but Jesse calls and offers his assistance. A year later, Jesse receives some much-needed support from Bob. Like the angels of Jacob's ladder, we are one interconnected spiritual chain, reaching up to a higher ground.

There are many ways to give. You can give of your time, your money, your talents, or yourself. There are many people to whom you can give—your family, friends, or those in the human family whom you do not know. It doesn't matter how you do it; the principle is the same. Every time you extend yourself outward, the universe extends itself to you. Whenever you put another first, the universe puts you first. The more you give, the more you receive.

Strive to reach out and and take the hand of the soul next to you. As you extend yourself in love, you will be uplifted to a new state of joyful awareness.

## *Affirmations*

1. The more I give to others, the more the universe gives to me.

2. There is enough to go around for everyone, including me.

3. Divine love in me blesses all that I am, all that I give, and all that I receive.

4. My cup runs over. I have **more** than I need, and so I share with my world.

5. Every dollar I contribute to others comes back to me multiplied.

6. Your own _____

_____

**Words To Consider**
*"You can have everything you want,*
*if you just help enough other people get what they want."*
Zig Ziglar

# TEN

# Everyone is your teacher

In the school of life, everything that happens to you is a teaching, and everyone is your teacher. Think of your experiences as coded messages that are saying, "There is something that you have to learn in order to grow and to expand."

An excellent example is illness. When you catch a cold or the flu, the universe is often saying, "Slow down! Take it easy; go inside for a while—you need to rest and focus on your inner world." If you pay attention to these messages, the universe will only nudge you when it wants your attention; if you ignore the small hints, life will confront you in the form of a crisis.

The most important of life's lessons come through other people—specifically those closest to you—parents, children, spouse, friends, and co-workers. Through these close relationships you learn the most valuable lessons of all—love, patience, sacrifice, generosity, and forgiveness.

Often your most significant teachings arise from those individuals and situations that are the most difficult. Look around at your life. Who or what is presenting you with the most problems? How are you responding to this challenge? Instead of remaining angry or frustrated, bless the situation or person. Ask that Higher wisdom reveal the meaning of the experience and lead you to a healing.

Every experience in life provides you with a special gift. Ask to receive it, and the gift will be yours.

# *Affirmations*

1.  Everyone is my teacher.

2.  I learn something valuable from each person I meet.

3.  I rejoice that I am continually being given the opportunity to grow in love.

4.  There are no bad experiences—only chances to learn.

5.  Divine wisdom reveals the inner meaning of each of my experiences.

6.  Your own _____

_____

**Words To Consider**
*"Life is a school;*
*Why not try taking the curriculum?"*
Proverb

# ELEVEN

# Heaven on earth

Oftentimes you may wonder, "What can I do to bring peace and harmony in the world?" The answer is clear—bring heaven down to earth.

Creating heaven on earth means shining light into your world, taking the mundane and making it sacred. Your spiritual path has provided you with a set of principles by which to live your daily life. Now is the time to become a **living example** of those principles until every aspect of your life is an expression of Divine love.

In prior times, those who wished to work on their spiritual development retreated from the world—entering monasteries and cloisters. But now, we are being called upon to fully immerse ourselves in the world in order to transform and heal the planet. We are called to be *in* the world but not *of* the world.

As you channel the qualities of spirit into your daily life, you will draw to yourself other people who are doing the same. Gradually, you will realize that this process is forming a chain reaction so that, one soul at a time, the entire globe is experiencing a spiritual rebirth.

Rejoice, for the time of awakening is at hand.

# Affirmations

1. I am a channel for Infinite Intelligence to do its work on earth.

2. Every one of my experiences brings me closer to God.

3. Higher wisdom expresses itself in all aspects of my daily life.

4. My inner peace enfolds the entire planet.

5. My life is a perfect demonstration of the principle of Divine love.

6. Your own _____

_____

**Words To Consider**
*"To see a world in a grain of sand and heaven in a wild flower,
Hold infinity in the palm of your hand and eternity in an hour."*
William Blake

# TWELVE

# According to your belief

How many times have you affirmed some good that you desired, (a fulfilling relationship, a better job, a new home, etc.), but never received it? This is because **deep inside**, you believed that you weren't worthy. According to your belief, so it is done unto you.

Think of the universe as an ocean. You may approach the ocean for water with a teaspoon or a bucket. The ocean in its vastness doesn't care what vessel you use or how much you take from it. It has more nourishment to give than you could ever require. What defines the amount of water you receive is the size of the container that you bring. What defines your supply is what you can accept in your innermost heart.

Ask yourself, "What am I bringing to my universe? Is it a teaspoon, a bucket, or a ten-gallon jar? What led me to decide which container I am using? *What do I think I deserve?*"

The universe wants to provide for your every need. Your task is to uncover and transform those limiting beliefs that have prevented you from accepting the good that is your birthright. To do this, you must learn to love yourself as much as you are loved by the Divine.

When you have achieved this self–love, then success, prosperity, and abundance will open before you.

# *Affirmations*

1. I am worthy to receive the unlimited offerings of the universe.

2. I claim my inheritance of Divine love and abundance.

3. I am changing and transforming my old and limiting beliefs.

4. I deserve to be prosperous and successful.

5. I deserve to be happy. I deserve love.

6. Your own _____
_____

**Words To Consider**
*"They can, because they think they can."*
Virgil

# THIRTEEN

# Feel your feelings

Feel your feelings. It seems like such a natural thing to do. Yet, many of us hold our feelings back. Perhaps we were criticized when we expressed them as a child. Maybe we are afraid that we will become overwhelmed and lose control.

But there is a better way, a better approach. It is based upon a universal rule about feelings:

When you **experience** feelings, they disappear; the more you resist them, the more they persist.

There are no good or bad feelings. A feeling is just a feeling. The so-called "negative" ones—anger, fear, hurt, sadness, grief and despair—are not harmful. It is only your acceptance or rejection of them that causes you to think in these terms.

Relax now and let some old feelings come up to the surface. As you move **toward** the emotions—watch them melt. If discomfort arises, use your pain as a meditation. Breathe into it. Surrender to it, and watch it transform.

As you go through this process and release blocked emotions from the past, you will experience a greater vitality in your body and spirit. Because you are not expending extra energy to deaden the pain, you will feel more alive than ever before. You will be a clearer and more open channel for the creative power that is within you.

# *Affirmations*

1. All of my feelings are valid.

2. I feel good when I feel.

3. It is safe to feel my feelings.

4. My feelings give me vitality, energy and strength.

5. I joyfully move toward my feelings, knowing they are my friends.

6. Your own _____

_____

**Words To Consider**
*"Emotions are like waves.*
*Watch them come and go on the vast ocean of existence."*
Proverb

# FOURTEEN

# Prosperity/Abundance

Look out to the natural world that surrounds you—the bountiful earth, the vast oceans, the expansive sky, the infinity of stars. You live in an abundant universe.

Where does this abundance come from? It comes from the creative power that formed the universe—from God, Infinite Intelligence, Divine spirit. The awareness of this intelligence as it exists within you is the key to experiencing abundance in your personal life. Since your connection to this source is unlimited, your potential supply is also unlimited.

The main factor that limits your supply is how much you think you deserve. A lack of prosperity in your life often reflects your limiting beliefs about what is possible. Perhaps you believe in a world of scarcity. You think, "There is only so much to go around. If I have more, others will have less." But the physical world manifests from creative thought, and since creative thought is limitless, so is the potential supply—for you and for everyone else.

Abundance is your birthright. Open yourself to the prosperity that you deserve. The pleasures of the physical world are yours to enjoy so long as you don't make them your master.

## *Affirmations*

1.  I believe in God as the source of my infinite supply which manifests through my life as abundance and prosperity on all levels.

2.  God-in-me is my unlimited and overflowing supply of every kind of good.

3.  I have more than I need, and so I share with my world.

4.  My prosperity contributes to the prosperity and well-being of others.

5.  The universe provides for my every want and need.

6.  Your own 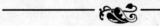 _____

_____

—— ❦ ——

**Words To Consider**
*"The only thing you will take through those pearly gates
is what you've given away."*
Marcia Moore

# FIFTEEN

# Growth through pain

While the fruits of the spiritual life are joy, love, peace, and harmony, one must also face tests and challenges, and overcome inner and outer temptations. How else can we develop our spiritual muscles unless we use them?

Pain is a marvelous feedback mechanism provided by the universe. Pain tells you that something is out of balance in your life, and that you must make the necessary changes to restore that balance.

Pain also helps you to develop a closer relationship with God. They say in Alcoholics Anonymous that one has to hit rock bottom before he or she is ready to be helped. It is the same for you. In times of despair, when you realize that your own efforts can no longer sustain you, you become **open** to asking for help from that Higher Power. And it is in these moments that you can hear the inner voice responding, "I am here with you always, even unto the end of the world."

Think back to the times in your life that were the most painful, the most difficult. Recall those moments when you suffered or lost the most. Consider what you *learned* from these occurrences; evaluate the growth that you experienced. Are you not a more compassionate, wise and understanding person as a result of what you went through?

Compare this to a time when all was going well, when your feelings of pain were at a minimum. Which of the experiences produced the greater growth and transformation in your life?

Invariably it will be the "painful" situation that has truly blessed you, that has opened your heart and made you a more loving human being.

## *Affirmations*

1   I thank the universe for providing me with opportunities to grow and to transform.

2.  A broken heart is an open heart; my heart has indeed been opened by my pain.

3.  I am a stronger and wiser person because of my tests and challenges.

4.  Better the pain, than to remain the same.

5.  I see all problems as disguised opportunities.

6.  Your own _____

_____

**Words To Consider**
*"The depth of darkness to which you can descend and still live is an exact measure of the height to which you can aspire to reach."*
Laurens Van der Post

# SIXTEEN

# A broken heart is an open heart

There is no pain quite like that of a broken heart. The experience of loss in love wounds us like no other. In the midst of our pain, we cry out, wishing there were something to take the hurt away. But there is nothing. There is no cure for a broken heart except for that universal healer, time.

If there is no cure for a broken heart, neither is there a guaranteed way to avoid having one. The more you risk, the more people you grow to love, the more it is possible that you will experience a separation. Yet, whenever your heart is broken, you receive a blessing—your broken heart becomes an open heart.

When we experience sadness and grief, something unexpected emerges. When we allow ourselves to be broken, a gentle transformation takes place. In the midst of the pain, we feel a softness and vulnerability that are truly beautiful. We become more accepting and open. Judgment and criticism are replaced by a compassion for others and an acceptance of life the way it is.

Think back to a time when your heart was broken. Remember what it was like to feel sadness and grief. Remember how your heart was opened. If you did not experience this opening then, see if you can allow it to happen now.

You were born to grow in love and understanding. By keeping your heart open and allowing it to experience both joy and pain, you will fulfill your highest destiny as a human being.

## *Affirmations*

1. I open myself to love.

2. I am willing to risk myself in love.

3. My vulnerability is my strength.

4. I open myself to loving and supportive relationships.

5. A broken heart is an open heart; when my heart breaks, I become more loving.

6. Your own _____

_____

**Words To Consider**
*"'Tis better to have loved and lost*
*than never to have loved at all."*
Tennyson

# SEVENTEEN

# Listen to yourself

We live in a world that is undergoing rapid transformation. The old rules and guidelines are no longer valid. There is only one source of information and guidance that you can depend upon—the voice of divinity within you.

The prophet Elijah was instructed to go to a mountain top to speak with God. When he arrived, he discovered that the Divine presence was not in the earthquake, nor in the wind, nor in the fire, but in "a still small voice." It is the same for you now. You can access that inner voice once you get quiet and listen.

When you first begin to listen, you may hear competing voices—the voices of your programming and conditioning from the past. How can you distinguish between them and the voice of your Higher Self? The key is to act on what you hear and observe what happens.

When the voice you follow is truly that of your intuition, you will experience more energy and vitality. Doors will open for you where you would not have expected them. A deep peace will accompany you in all that you do.

If, however, you have followed an inauthentic voice, you will experience confusion instead of clarity, blocks instead of flow, depletion instead of vitality. Then it is time to go back inside and listen again.

You know what is best for you. Listen to yourself. There is no one else to follow.

# *Affirmations*

1. I am a clear and open channel for the power of the universe.

2. I am constantly attuned to the voice of Divinity within me.

3. I listen to myself and confidently act upon what I hear.

4. As I act on my intuition, Divine order appears in all parts of my life.

5. When I follow my inner voice, the universe supports and nurtures me.

6. Your own _____

_____

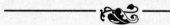

**Words To Consider**
*"Let us be silent, that we may hear the whispers of the Gods."*
Emerson

# EIGHTEEN

# Words that heal

Throughout the ages, mystics have recognized the power of the spoken word to bring ideas into physical manifestation. As the first verse in the Gospel of John proclaims, "In the beginning was the *word*." This is why affirmations are so powerful. Through the repetition of a word or phrase, you create a magnetic field that attracts the desired condition to you.

If you knew the power of your words, you would be very careful about what you say. In a moment of discouragement, have you ever thought, "Why is it that I can't succeed? Why can't I ever seem to get what I want?" Such negative self-talk creates the very condition you are trying to avoid. As the prophet tells us, "Thou art ensnared by the words of thy mouth."

When we talk negatively about other people, our words have a detrimental effect on all concerned. Perhaps this is why our parents told us, "If you can't say something positive about someone, then don't say anything at all."

Words are very potent; they can be used to create a variety of outcomes. There are words that hurt, and words that heal. Take inventory now, and ask yourself, "What am I talking up in my life? What am I affirming?"

There is creative power in your every word. Use that power to draw the very best into your life and into the lives of others.

# *Affirmations*

1.  I affirm only the best for myself and others.

2.  My words are positive, healing and nurturing.

3.  I use the creative power of my words to manifest the good that I desire.

4.  My word is my wand, attracting to me all good things.

5.  I feast on positive words and ideas. I fast from negative thinking.

6.  Your own _____

_____

**Words To Consider**
*"Keep your words sweet, in case you have to eat them."*
Proverb

# NINETEEN

# Guidance

During a time of transition, many of us look for reliable ways to receive guidance and direction in our lives. But with our familiar signposts in chaos and turmoil, there is only one certain way to obtain the guidance we seek—go within.

In seeking guidance, you are really asking the universe to "show you the way." A lovely way to request this direction is to affirm, **"I want to do what God wants me to do."** This statement will cause your Higher wisdom to communicate its intention to you. Then, your task is simple—listen to and follow its instructions.

Sometimes, what you receive will be different from what you (your ego) wants to hear. Don't let this bother you; your intuition, not your ego, knows what's best for you. At other times, your instructions will not "make sense." Again, don't be concerned; your intuition doesn't function through logic, but through what "feels" right.

When you receive guidance, rather than being shown the final outcome, you will probably be told to take a single step. This is where you must exercise your faith. Trust that you are being led in the right direction and that everything will work out. The universe wants you to succeed. The universe wants the best for you.

As you repeat this procedure, your guidance will become clearer and more defined. With each new day, you will experience the security and inner calm that come through following your Higher Power.

# Affirmations

1. I want to do what the universe wants me to do.

2. I want to do what my Higher Self wants me to do.

3. The Divine Presence fills my body, mind, heart and soul. From this place of higher knowing, I see all things clearly.

4. God's wisdom illumines me, shining light on my path.

5. All things are working together for good in my life.

6. Your own _____

   _____

**Words To Consider**
*"The Lord is nigh to all who call upon him,*
*to all who call upon him in truth."*
Psalm 145:18

# TWENTY

# Count your blessings

Everyone alive has problems. These challenges stimulate us to grow and to transform. But in focusing on what's "wrong" with our lives, we often forget what's right.

In fact, there is a great deal that is right. Consider your health. Your body is a marvelous temple that allows you to experience the miracle of life. Yet, most of the time, you take it for granted.

If you have a loving family, a fulfilling primary relationship, or a close friendship, you are fortunate indeed!

And what about your material circumstances? Perhaps you may not be able to afford everything you want, but you probably have food to eat, clothes to wear, and a roof over your head.

Turn to your own life and count your blessings. Take inventory of all that you have to be thankful for. Ask yourself, "What good in my life have I been taking for granted?" No matter how many challenges you are facing, you can find some aspect of your life for which to be grateful.

One at a time, review your blessings. Perhaps you might want to write them down and affirm them. As you take stock of these riches, you will feel a lightness of heart that comes from knowing how blessed you truly are.

# *Affirmations*

1. I give thanks for the many blessings that I experience in my life.

2. I am blessed in all ways.

3. My life overflows with every kind of good.

4. I am endowed with abundant health, wealth, love and creative self-expression.

5. I give thanks that the universe is fully supporting me.

6. Your own _____
_____

**Words To Consider**
*"Count your blessings, not your crosses,
Count your gains, not your losses.
Count your joys instead of your woes,
Count your friends instead of your foes.
Covet your health, not your wealth."*
Proverb

# TWENTY ONE

# The universe wants the best for you

The Infinite Intelligence in which we live, move and have our being is essentially good. Or, as the apostle John puts it, "God is love, and he who dwells in love dwells in God." This is not to deny the existence of evil or negativity. But, there is a loving force in which you can take refuge, one that will do its utmost to provide for and protect you each step along the path.

An ancient spiritual law states that every challenge, difficulty, or defeat contains within it the seed of an equivalent or **greater** good. To receive the gift, ask that it be revealed to you. Once you learn to look for the good in life, you will experience **every** situation as promoting your spiritual growth and development.

The universe wants the best for you. It will give to and support you, if you allow it to do so. Sometimes you may have to leave a known situation (your job, home, relationship, etc.) for the unknown in order to move forward with your life. If you find yourself overwhelmed by fear, repeat the affirmation "The universe wants the best for me." Then, step out in faith, and give life the opportunity to support you. If you keep your focus on that Higher Power, all the details will fall into place.

Because you are a child of Love, all things are working together for your highest good. It cannot be otherwise.

# *Affirmations*

1. The world is a safe and nurturing place.

2. The universe has made ample provision for every need in my life.

3. My cup runneth over.

4. I am guided and protected at all times and in all places.

5. When I follow my heart, the universe supports me, both spiritually and materially.

6. Your own _____

_____

**Words To Consider**
*"Everything serves to further."*
The Book of Changes

# TWENTY TWO

# The challenge of change

Life is speeding up. With the emergence of the scientific revolution in the late 1700's, the rate of change on our planet began to accelerate. We are now moving with great speed into a new era of consciousness and awareness.

Everything is in a state of flux; nothing is immune to this change. No one knows what will happen from one day to the next. Each of us is on his own, having only the universe as a guide.

How are you responding to these times of accelerated change? Are you hanging on to the past, or are you going with the flow? If you are attempting to fight the universe, you are trying to swim upstream against a swift, powerful current. Why not let go and allow the river to carry you?

As you raise your vibrations in concert with the universal flow, every cell in your body is transforming. Lessons which took weeks, months and even years to learn are occurring in a matter of days or hours.

Look back upon your life. You are not the same person you were last year, or even last week. Your old habits and negative thought forms are being released and replaced. Yes, you are being changed in the "twinkling of an eye."

Rejoice, for these are exciting and wondrous times. Evolution is about to take a quantum leap forward. Open yourself to this change, and let it carry you into a glorious future.

## *Affirmations*

1. I let go, and let the universe guide me.

2. I welcome change into my life.

3. Every day and every way, I am getting better and better.

4. I release the past to make way for a glorious present.

5. I am changing, growing and moving forward in consciousness.

6. Your own _____

_____

**Words To Consider**
*"Behold, I show you a mystery.*
*We shall not all sleep, but we shall all be changed."*
I Corinthians 15:51

# TWENTY THREE

# Patience

Anything worthwhile in life requires time and patience. Think of all in your life that you treasure—a relationship with your spouse, the raising of your child, mastering the piano, winning an award. These achievements took time to accomplish.

Nature is the same way. Observe how long natural forces take to accomplish their handiwork. The Colorado River spent thousands of centuriess carving out its majestic sculpture, the Grand Canyon. The beautiful Appalachian mountains have been 230 million years in the making.

When we attempt to achieve something worthwhile, we very rarely succeed on our first try. Abraham Lincoln lost four elections before he became president. Thomas Edison made 2,000 attempts at the light bulb before he succeeded. Because they had faith in themselves, these individuals kept pursuing their dreams until they emerged victorious.

You have heard of the patience of Job. His was a patience based upon faith. It is the same with you. If you are experiencing delays right now, keep *your* faith. Stay true to yourself. Move forward in the direction of your dreams, keeping your eyes fixed on your goal until your vision takes form. In the end, such persistence will lead you to your heart's desire.

# *Affirmations*

1. My persistence and determination work miracles.

2. Delays give me time to prepare for the good that awaits me.

3. I'm hanging in there.

4. Once I begin a project, I have the patience and endurance to finish the task.

5. Every setback makes me more determined to reach my objectives.

6. Your own _____

_____

**Words To Consider**
*"They that wait upon the Lord shall renew their strength.*
*They shall run and not be weary;*
*They shall walk and not faint."*
Isaiah 40:31

# TWENTY FOUR

# Love yourself

All love begins with self-love. Before others can drink from your cup, it must first be filled. When the cup runs dry, it is you who can best replenish it.

Loving yourself means giving your body the food, exercise and rest that it needs. It means listening to your feelings and asking others for what you want—without feeling guilty about it.

Loving yourself also means praising yourself, giving yourself pats on the back. It means stopping your self-criticism and self-judgment, and accepting yourself the way you are.

Loving yourself means taking care of yourself by putting your needs **first**, if that is what it takes to maintain your wholeness. As you take care of your own needs, you will be better able to meet the needs of your friends and loved ones.

Loving yourself means becoming a parent to your inner child. When that child gets upset, give it some love and nurturance. Take yourself out to dinner or treat yourself to a healing massage. Once you begin to give to yourself, it will become natural to share this giving with others.

Love your neighbor **as yourself.** How often we focus on the "neighbor" but forget the "self." As you learn to love and accept yourself, your inner light will shine outward to bless and heal your fellow human beings.

## *Affirmations*

1. I love and accept myself just the way I am.

2. I love myself unconditionally.

3. Universal love fills and surrounds every cell of my being.

4. The more I love myself, the more I love others.

5. My life overflows with the bounties of love.

6. Your own _____
_____

**Words To Consider**
" *When the flower blooms, the bees come uninvited.* "
Ramakrishna

# TWENTY FIVE

# Enjoy the journey

Life is a journey, not a destination. Life is a *process* that is experienced in the here and now, in the eternal present. What is the quality of your daily life? Are you having **fun** in what you are pursuing? If you are not enjoying yourself, it may not be worth it.

At times you may say, "When I have reached the *end* of my journey—when I get married, when the baby arrives, when I get the new job, when I finally retire—**then I will be happy**." In the meantime, you have missed out on the essence of life—living.

Planning for the future has its place. It is important to set goals and pursue them. But while you are striving to reach your desired end, be open to those experiences of pleasure, beauty, peace and tranquility. Take time to appreciate life's precious moments. Take time to enjoy the journey.

Allow your direction to come straight from the Divine. Moment by moment, breath by breath, guidance will be revealed if you turn within. You are living in a new era where there is no pattern to follow. There are no more maps, no more creeds, no more philosophies to depend upon. Everything is subject to change.

Therefore, be flexible. Trust your inner source to guide you each step along the way. Relax and enjoy the journey.

# Affirmations

1. I enjoy myself and the people around me.

2. The quality of my life is superb.

3. I am having fun.

4. I am divinely guided.

5. I am at peace with myself and the universe.

6. Your own _____
   _____

**Words To Consider**
*"The greatest of God's angels is Joy.*
*She leans over us and gives us the secret of eternity, which is Love.*
*I used to weep that all did not share."*
Norman Lee

# TWENTY SIX

# You make a difference

Everyone needs to feel he or she is having an impact. Everyone needs to know that he or she makes a difference in the world. But in our complex and vast society, you may often wonder if you count at all.

The fact is that you do make a difference—an incredible difference—by the way you live your life each day. Your deeds may not get reported in *Time* magazine, but, far from being insignificant, they have a tremendous influence on the world.

Consider the following example. A shoeshine man in a St. Louis airport does his job with such love that he uplifts everyone who walks past him. People waiting for their planes literally surround him in order to bask in his light.

You may experience these examples in your own life. The clerk at the check-out stand makes your day with a smile; a stranger stops to help you fix a flat tire; a dedicated teacher transforms the lives of countless students who pass through her classroom. These, and millions of individuals like them, are changing the world.

No man is an island. We live in an interconnected universe. This is not just some metaphysical notion; it is a physical fact. Like a radio transmitter, you transmit your thought waves to all corners of the universe. Every action that you take and every thought that you think has an impact.

You make a difference.

# *Affirmations*

1. I make a difference in the world.

2. I am an important person.

3. I feel my connection to the universe.

4. I have an impact on those around me.

5. I am the light of the world. I let my light shine for all to see.

6. Your own _____
_____

**Words To Consider**
*"No act of kindness, however small, is ever wasted."*
Proverb

# TWENTY SEVEN

# You have the power

There is tremendous power residing within you. As you become aware of the truth of who you really are, this power will stir and slowly awaken.

Getting in touch with your power comes from acknowledging yourself as being at cause in your life. You are the creator, not the created. You, not your neighbor, are responsible for your life. Once you understand this, you will be able to create whatever support you need in life.

In our culture, we are often conditioned to feel powerless and helpless. Rather than take responsibility for our lives, we blame outside forces—"He did it to me; she did it to me, the world did it to me." But, as Eleanor Roosevelt reminded us, "Nobody has the ability to oppress you unless you give them permission." Even when you are surrounded by negativity, you have the power to program your mind to receive only the good.

The final step in realizing your power comes when you align your will with the Higher will. With the full force of the universe behind you, you can achieve results that transcend your normal limitations. Of course, this power can only be used for the highest good of all concerned.

Become a selfless channel for good and let the universe work miracles through you.

# *Affirmations*

1. I have the ability to create support for myself in my life.

2. God-in-me is my strength.

3. I can do all things through the power of God within me.

4. I am confident, self-assured, and optimistic.

5. I am the creator of my life and my world.

6. Your own _____

_____

**Words To Consider**
*"He can who thinks he can,*
*And he can't who thinks he can't.*
*This is an indisputable law."*
Henry Ford

# TWENTY EIGHT

# Feel the fear and proceed anyway

The greatest obstacle to your spiritual progress and well-being is FEAR. Fear is an emotion that can protect you from real danger, but most of your fears are self-created. Fear paralyzes you into inaction, or worse yet, becomes a self-fulfilling prophecy. As Job discovered, "The thing that I feared most has come upon me."

One method of dealing with fear is courage. Courage is not the absence of fear, but the *willingness* to move forward in spite of the fear. You acknowledge the fear and take action anyway.

Another antidote to fear is is to turn yourself over to a Higher Power. A recovering alcoholic spoke of having released the fear in her life after she entrusted her cares to God. The psalmist David writes of a similar experience in the 23rd Psalm. "Though I walk through the valley of the shadow of death, I will fear no evil: for thou art with me; thy rod and thy staff they comfort me."

A third remedy is to invoke the state of love within yourself. Love and fear cannot exist side by side. As it is written, "Perfect love casts out fear."

It is fine to experience your fears. Acknowledge them, appreciate them. And then move forward in courage, faith, and love.

# *Affirmations*

1. My life is unfolding perfectly.

2. The Lord is my shepherd; I shall not want.

3. I say good-bye to my past fears.

4. If God is for me, who can be against me?

5. I live in a safe and nurturing world.

6. Your own _____

_____

**Words To Consider**
*"The only thing we have to fear is fear itself."*
Franklin D. Roosevelt

# TWENTY NINE

# Do what you love:
# the universe will provide

The path of the heart is the path of power. Anything you do out of love will heal and uplift you. Following your heart's desire will also draw whatever resources you need to support your endeavors.

A writer created a book because he wanted to share a subject he loved. The book was published and did modestly well. Encouraged, he came up with an idea that he knew was a money-maker, but did not come from his heart. His sole reason for writing the book was to make a profit. But because the work lacked authenticity, it sold poorly. Consequently, he decided to return to a subject that inspired him. The resulting book became an unexpected success.

The moral of this story is clear: Risk going after what you really want in your life. Give the universe a chance to support you. You won't know until you try.

Start with small steps. Listen to your intuition. Identify what you love to do, and begin pursuing it. Gradually expand those activities until they involve more of your time. As your creative energy opens up, notice the increase in your aliveness, vitality, and finances.

Eventually, your entire life will become an expression of love in action.

# Affirmations

1. When I trust myself and the universe, anything is possible.

2. God has great things in store for me.

3. As I follow my heart's desire, I draw whatever I need to me.

4. The more I trust my intuition, the more prosperity comes my way.

5. I am amply rewarded for my creative ideas.

6. Your own _____

_____

**Words To Consider**

*"If a man does not keep pace with his companions,*
*perhaps it is because he hears a different drummer.*
*Let him step to the music which he hears,*
*however measured or far away."*
Thoreau

# THIRTY

# Give thanks for all things

Thankfulness is one of the key ingredients for our progress along the path. So often we lose sight of what we have to be grateful for—our health, friends, material comfort, and most important, the gift of life itself.

Every situation in life, even the apparent tragedy, has a "silver lining." Giving thanks invokes this good and helps to bring it into being. Even painful experiences become bitter-sweet when the universe works out its perfect plan through them.

A woman friend underwent a very painful breakup with someone she loved. From a logical point of view, the experience was a horrible trauma. Everything she cherished was ripped away; the pain seemed unbearable. Nonetheless, she gave thanks.

Many years passed before the wounds healed. Then she met a new partner. The relationship flourished and brought a level of joy and fulfillment that had been lacking in the old. The breakup, she realized, was truly a gift.

Take a look at your life. Are you giving thanks for *all* your experiences? If you are reacting negatively to a specific situation, try a different approach.

Give thanks for the condition being just the way it is. Then observe what happens. As your attitude about the condition changes, the circumstances surrounding it will be transformed. Such is the miraculous power of giving thanks for all things.

---

## *Affirmations*

1. I give thanks for every experience that I have.

2. I say "yes" to the universe.

3. It's all unfolding perfectly.

4. Every experience in my life brings me closer to God.

5. In every aspect of my life, I am truly blessed.

6. Your own _____
   _____

**Words To Consider**
*"When you learn to love hell, you will be in heaven."*
Proverb

# THIRTY ONE

# This too shall pass

According to an ancient tale, a Sufi village was attacked and captured by a group of warriors. The king of the victorious tribe called the Sufi leaders and said that unless they could tell him what would make him "happy when he was sad, and sad when he was happy," the entire village would be put to death the following morning.

The village people constructed a large bonfire, and all night long their wise men and women strove to answer the king's question: What could make a person happy when he is sad, and sad when he is happy? Finally, sunrise came and the king entered the village. Approaching the wise ones he asked, "Have you fulfilled my request?" One of the wise men then reached into a pouch and presented the king with a gold ring. The king was perplexed. "I have no need of more gold," he exclaimed. "How can this ring make me happy when I am sad, and sad when I am happy?" Then the king looked again and saw an inscription. It read "**This too shall pass**."

So it is in your life. When everything is going according to plan, savor those precious moments and realize that in time they will be a distant memory. And when the night is darkest and you can't imagine things ever improving, remember that nothing in the physical world lasts forever.

In this way, you will learn to accept both the good and bad times equally, understanding that **all** of life's teachings are necessary for your spiritual growth. With this realization, you will be like the great saint who proclaimed, "One to me is Loss and Gain, one to me is Pleasure and Pain, one to me is Fame and Shame."

## *Affirmations*

1. Rather than seek pleasure and avoid pain, I accept both as having equal benefit.

2. What goes up must come down.

3. What goes down must come up.

4. Time and love can heal *all* of my wounds.

5. My old pains no longer hurt me. They have become a distant memory.

6. Your own _____

_____

### Words To Consider
*"Remember, no human condition is ever permanent. Then you will not be overjoyed in good fortune nor too sorrowful in misfortune."*
Socrates

# THIRTY TWO

# Death be not proud

Of all the aspects of existence that we contemplate, death is the most baffling. Although it signifies an ending of the known, is it really a finality? The great mystic Paracelsus said "What is death? It is the annihilation of the form, but not of **life**. It is the separation of the immortal from the mortal part of us. It is that which returns us to the life we left when we were born."

Death is an ongoing process. The apostle Paul proclaimed, "I die daily." A single life contains thousands of emotional deaths. A friend moves away. Your child graduates from school. You leave a job for a position in a new company. You sell your home and buy another. Each of these transitions is a death.

Every day of your life, millions of cells die while millions more take their place. You are no longer the same person you were yesterday or last week. How many times have you died? How many lives have you lived in this lifetime alone?

So really death is about *change*, the only constant in life. A state far worse than death is stagnation—staying stuck and not growing or moving forward. It is this condition, not death, that you must avoid.

The change you call "death," therefore, can only serve to further you along your path. There is nothing to fear. Death is an ally that will transform your existence from a caterpillar to that of a glorious butterfly.

## *Affirmations*

1. I die and am transformed daily.

2. Each death leads me to a glorious rebirth.

3. I embrace change, knowing that it transforms my life.

4. When one door closes, another door opens.

5. Better the pain than to remain the same.

6. Your own 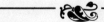 _____

_____

**Words To Consider**
*"The reports of my death are greatly exaggerated."*
Mark Twain

# THIRTY THREE

# Transforming our world

The earth and all humanity are entering a new age, a new cycle of evolution. This rebirth is characterized by a change of consciousness from isolation and separation to unity and oneness. The transformation is not limited to any age, religion, culture, race or nationality. It is a global experience that is leading to the creation of a planetary culture.

Although the effects of this process are being felt on the mass level, the change is taking place one person at a time, as seen in the story about the little boy whose father cut up a picture of a globe from the daily newspaper and asked him to put the pieces together. Five minutes later the boy returned with the globe perfectly rearranged. The father asked, "How did you put the world together so easily?" "It was simple," the boy replied. "On the other side of the world was a picture of a man. When I got the man together, the world came together."

More and more people are "getting themselves together," releasing old thoughts of fear and separation and replacing them with thoughts of love and unity. When a small but significant number of people (known as the "critical mass") reaches this new level of awareness, the change will be experienced by all of humanity.

This is how the world will be transformed. You have your part to play. Because your consciousness is connected to the planetary whole, as you change, the world around you will change. In fact, you might provide the tiny "push" that shifts the balance and ushers in the beginning of a glorious new era.

## *Affirmations*

1.  The world is experiencing a planetary rebirth.

2.  As I heal myself, the planet becomes healed.

3.  We are one interconnected, interdependent world.

4.  I see myself as a planetary citizen.

5.  I live in a global village whose residents are my brothers and sisters.

6.  Your own _____

_____

**Words To Consider**
*"No man is an island, entire of itself;*
*every man is a piece of the continent, a part of the main."*
John Donne

# THIRTY FOUR

# It's all unfolding perfectly

Whenever you feel that life has given you more than you can deal with, remember the cosmic law "It's all unfolding perfectly." The universe never gives you more than you are able to handle. Even those events that seem to thwart you are actually helping you to fulfill your destiny.

In many instances, this way of viewing life may be obvious. At other times, you may feel that life is cursing, not blessing you. When this occurs, realize that your view of the situation is limited.

Science tells us that we see only a small portion of the existing light waves. The major part of the electromagnetic spectrum remains invisible to us. On the spiritual path, you likewise see only a small slice of the soul's unfoldment. If you could get up high enough to see the whole picture, your current predicament would make sense. You would discover why you have chosen your particular challenges and how to resolve them.

Fortunately, there is a way for you to see the "big picture"—get in touch with your Higher Self through prayer and meditation. From this elevated vantage point, you will gain a new perspective on life. You will see that at every moment you draw to yourself *exactly* what you need for your highest development. Even when you don't know how it all fits together, you will hear an inner voice that says "Trust in the process. It's all unfolding perfectly."

# *Affirmations*

1. It's all unfolding perfectly.

2. I say "yes" to my universe.

3. All things are working together for good in my life.

4. Whatever I am ready for is ready for me.

5. There are no accidents. Everything happens
   for a reason.

6. Your own _____

_____

**Words To Consider**
*"God, grant me the ability to accept the things I cannot change,*
*The courage to change the things I can,*
*And the wisdom to know the difference."*
Reinhold Niebuhr

# THIRTY FIVE

# The silver lining

Every cloud, no matter how dark, contains a silver lining. Good can emerge from *any* situation. Look for this gift, and search until you have found it.

The law of compensation states that every situation or event contains within it both the good and the bad, the pleasant and the painful; even the most wonderful situation contains pain when we realize that it cannot last. When you focus on the positive aspect of any situation, you help to bring it into manifestation. By looking for the good, you cause it to happen.

A college baseball player was injured and forced to sit out the season. At first he was quite upset about his apparent misfortune. The next year, however, the team's chemistry came together and he led them to the championship. Looking back to the difficult times, he reflected, "I know this sounds crazy, but I'm actually glad I got injured. It was the best thing that could have happened to me."

Begin now to practice seeing the silver lining in every situation. Everything is working for your ultimate good. As you learn to look for that good, you will experience the best in every circumstance you encounter.

## *Affirmations*

1. Every one of my life experiences contains a valuable teaching.

2. Behind every dark cloud there lies a rainbow.

3. Every adversity brings me a wonderful teaching.

4. Whatever the problem, God reveals the perfect solution.

5. I learn from every situation I encounter.

6. Your own _____

_____

**Words To Consider**
*"My barn having burned to the ground,
I can now see the moon."*
Japanese Haiku

# THIRTY SIX

# Release

Are you holding on to a person, situation or resentment/hurt that you have harbored for many years? If so, now is the time to release. Now is the time to flush these old feelings from your system and relieve yourself of their psychic and spiritual burdens.

Imagine yourself standing before the person, circumstance or feeling that you wish to release. Visualize a slim silver thread running from your solar plexus to the person or situation. Now imagine the two of you slowly separating and repeat to yourself, "The divine in me blesses and releases the divine in you. The divine in me blesses and releases the divine in you." As this occurs, see the thread slowly stretching and unraveling until it breaks. You are free.

Some pain may surface during this exercise. Rather than push it away, surrender to it and flow with the experience. As you lessen your resistance to the pain, the pain itself will decrease. If you experience sadness, remember that sadness is the healing feeling. Sadness completes the past and allows you to move on.

When you have succeeded in letting go, a wonderful experience will come along to replace what you left behind. Have faith that a beautiful life awaits you. Be patient. Expect the best.

# *Affirmations*

1. I let go of the old and make way for the new.

2. I release my fears and insecurities and replace them with faith and confidence.

3. A great weight has been lifted from my shoulders.

4. I give thanks for my new life.

5. I bless and release all my old pain.

6. Your own _____

_____

**Words To Consider**
*"To everything there is a season,
and a time to every purpose under heaven.
A time to get and a time to lose;
a time to keep and a time to cast away."*
Ecclesiastes 3:1, 3:6

# THIRTY SEVEN

# Forgiveness

The greatest act of healing is the act of forgiveness. It is also the most difficult. An immutable law states, "As you forgive, so shall you be forgiven." Thus, forgiveness is an act of self-kindness. It may also heal the other person, but ultimately forgiveness is done for yourself.

People do harm only when they are in pain. If you continue to hate the person who hurt you, your resentment will bind you together; but if you transform your hatred into love, both of you will be free. This is why the great teachers have advised us to love our enemies.

Take a moment and hold someone in your mind's eye for whom you feel resentment. Now say to this individual "I forgive you. I forgive you for whatever you may have done in the past that caused me pain, intentionally or unintentionally—through your actions, your words, or your thoughts. However you may have caused me to suffer, I forgive you."

Allow this person to be touched by your forgiveness. For just an instant, move beyond the past and let your hearts touch in compassion and mercy. When you have finished, say good-bye and release them.

All forgiveness starts with self-forgiveness. Use this exercise to forgive yourself for the pain you have caused yourself or others. Let yourself back into your heart. Have mercy on yourself. Allow yourself to be forgiven. Allow yourself to be healed.

# *Affirmations*

1. I bless and release all those who have caused me pain.

2. I forgive everyone; I forgive myself; I let go of the past; I am free!

3. I forgive myself for whatever suffering I have caused myself or others.

4. I let myself back into my heart.

5. As I forgive, so am I forgiven.

6. Your own _____

_____

**Words To Consider**
*"To err is human, to forgive divine."*
Alexander Pope

# THIRTY EIGHT

# The divinity within

According to a Hindu legend, humans had so abused their divine powers that the gods decided to remove their divinity and hide it where men would never find it. But the question was, where? If they hid the divinity deep within the earth, men would dig down and uncover it. If they sank it in the deepest ocean, humans would eventually locate it on the ocean bed. If the divinity were placed on the highest mountain, one day people would scale the peak and find it there.

Finally, the wisest of the gods said, "Here is what we will do with man's divinity. We will hide it deep within man himself, for that is the last place he would ever think to look for it."

And so it has been. For centuries, we have been exploring the earth, sea and sky, searching for an experience that has resided in our own backyard. But now humanity is at a critical juncture. We are at last seeking the divinity within—where it has resided all along.

You are an important part of this transformation. As you begin to turn within, your spirituality will emerge from your experience of that inner divinity.

As more people realize the God within, the religious dogmas and conflicts that have divided the planet will disappear. No matter what culture or background we come from, our inner experience of the Divine will be one and the same.

It will be the experience of Love.

## *Affirmations*

1. The kingdom of God resides within me.

2. I have the answers to all of my questions.

3. The source of my contentment and joy lies inside.

4. My happiness is independent of outside events or circumstances.

5. I choose to experience peace of mind.


6. Your own _____

_____

**Words To Consider**
*"The kingdom of God cometh not by observation,
Neither shall they say, 'Look here!' or 'Look there!'
For behold, the kingdom of God is within you."*
Luke 17:20-21

# THIRTY NINE

# Healing your life

What is healing? The words *healing, health* and *holy* come from the same root—meaning **whole**. Healing is a quality of wholeness, completeness, and oneness.

Healing can occur on many levels—physical, mental, emotional or spiritual. Many times the true healing has little to do with the body's response. A woman who was dying of cancer used the opportunity to open her heart for the first time in her life. As a result, she healed her estranged relationship with her mother and daughter. Although the body died, her soul experienced a profound healing.

In another instance, a man who lost his spouse felt such pain that he was forced to reach out to his children. Through his grief, his pride and arrogance were washed away and replaced by an openness and humility.

In each of these instances, the experience of healing brought forth an opening of the heart to a new wholeness and completeness.

Take a moment and think of an area of your life that needs to be healed. Send love and blessings to that part of yourself. Ask that you may be led to the path of healing that you need. As you begin to heal yourself, you will also heal a portion of the planet.

Above all, realize that the true source of your healing is the divinity within. Although you must take the first step in striving for wholeness, it is God-in-you who does the healing.

## *Affirmations*

1.  My body is healed, restored, and filled with energy.

2.  Every day, in every way, I am getting better and better.

3.  I am restored and revitalized.

4.  God-in-me is my health, right now!

5.  I align my personal healing with the healing of the planet.

6.  Your own _____

_____

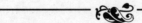

**Words To Consider**
*"The greatest thing in this world is not so much where we are,
but in what direction we are moving."*
Oliver Wendell Holmes

# FORTY

# The joy of laughter

Have you ever had a depressing thought in the middle of a good laugh? It's next to impossible. When you laugh, your brain produces natural mood elevators that miraculously free you from attachment to pain and suffering.

Laughter brings about a deep sense of *joy* and *peace* that is truly therapeutic. Humor not only transforms your mind and emotions, it can cure your body. People have healed themselves of chronic illnesses through introducing laughter into their lives. Now medical science is applying the healing power of humor to reduce stress and promote the body's recuperative powers.

Laughter also helps you to keep your life in its proper perspective. When you laugh at yourself, you learn to take yourself far less seriously. That is why angels can fly—because they take themselves so lightly.

Laughter is the shortest distance between two people. Think about your most treasured relationships. It's likely that you and your closest friends share a common sense of humor.

When was the last time you had a good laugh? If it has been a while, let your inner child come out and play. Watch your favorite comedy. Try seeing the cosmic humor in your situation. Having fun in life doesn't mean you're avoiding pain. Enjoy yourself!

## *Affirmations*

1. My personality is radiant with humor.

2. I'm laughing my way to enlightenment.

3. I haven't had this much fun in years.

4. People appreciate my sense of humor.

5. I just can't stop laughing.

6. Your own _____

_____

**Words To Consider**
*"He who laughs, lasts."*
Proverb

# FORTY ONE

# Think on these things

"As a man thinketh, so is he." "You become what you think about most of the time." These sayings express a fundamental truth—that thought is creative.

Look around at your physical environment. The chair on which you are sitting, the clothes you are wearing, the building that surrounds you—before these objects took on form, they began as an **idea** in someone's mind. That is precisely how all things manifest in the material world. They begin in the realm of thought.

Likewise, you create your own world through the thoughts that you think. You are the writer, director and star of your own movie. If you are dissatisfied with how the plot is unfolding, rewrite the script through changing your thoughts and beliefs. As the apostle Paul reminded us, "Be ye *transformed* by the renewing of your mind."

There is tremendous power in positive thinking. When you expect the best, you literally create a thought field that magnetizes that which you desire. Like attracts like. This force can also work against you, as Job discovered when he realized, "The thing that I feared most has come upon me."

It is up to you to jealously guard what goes into and comes out of your mind. There is plenty of negativity that would like to find a home within your psyche. See to it that only the good and the positive enter in.

# *Affirmations*

1. I fill my mind with positive, nurturing, and healing thoughts.

2. What I believe about myself is what I will become— and so I believe the best.

3. I can feel the sunshine, even when clouds are over-head.

4. My peaceful and tranquil thoughts relax and soothe every inch of my body.

5. I am transformed by the renewing of my mind.

6. Your own _____

_____

**Words To Consider**
*"All that we are is a result
of what we have thought."*
Abraham Lincoln

# FORTY TWO

# Judge not

Some of the most difficult thought patterns to transform are those of criticism and judgment. How many of us act upon the wisdom of the American Indian saying, "Let me not judge another person until I have walked a mile in his moccasins?" Open your heart, and allow your criticism to melt into compassion.

Often we criticize others in the hope that they will change. But the only person you can truly change is yourself. The only person you can save is you. Start at home. Look into your own heart. How much of what you judge in others is really an unacceptable aspect of yourself?

If you want to see change, begin by healing that wounded part of your psyche. Forgive yourself for your own failings. Remove the bias from your own eye, that you may see your neighbor more clearly.

Remember that *everyone*, including yourself, is doing the best he or she can. When you experience your neighbor's misfortune as your own, you will see his predicament in a new light. Having walked and blistered your feet in those tattered moccasins, you will at last be able to say, **"I understand."**

# *Affirmations*

1.  I judge no one, especially myself.

2.  Everyone, including myself, is doing the best he can.

3.  I accept myself as I am. I accept others as they are.

4.  My heart is open and filled with compassion.

5.  The greatest force in all of creation is the healing power of love. I align myself with that force.

6.  Your own _____

_____

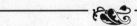

**Words To Consider**
*"Let me walk three weeks in the footsteps of my enemy,*
*carry the same burden, have the same trials as he,*
*before I say one word to criticize."*
An Indian Chief's prayer

# FORTY THREE

# Service

We were put on this earth to serve one another. Parents provide for their children, spouse supports spouse, friends help friends—life is sustained and nurtured through unconditional love and service.

Service is more than a one-way process. The more you freely give of yourself, the more you are given to give. Or, as Jesus put it, "He who would lose himself for My sake will find himself." Two months before his death, Martin Luther King, Jr. stated that the only possession he would have to leave behind was a "committed life." Twenty years later, a national holiday commemorates his legacy—a life of service.

There is always somebody for you to serve, and someone who is equally eager to assist you. The image of Jacob's ladder wonderfully illustrates the win-win nature of serving. Like the figures on the ladder, when we pull our neighbor upward, we are simultaneously lifted up by the person above us. By helping one another along, we can *all* reach our spiritual destination together.

Take a look at your own life. See yourself serving the planet and its inhabitants. It is of little importance how the world regards your contribution. What matters is the motivation behind your service. Smiling at a stranger promotes as much healing as discovering a new vaccine. No act of kindness, however small, is ever wasted.

## *Affirmations*

1. The more I give, the more I am given to give.

2. The more I give away, the more I receive.

3. Everywhere I look, I see opportunities to serve.

4. I give, simply for the joy of giving.

5. I wish success and good fortune to everyone I know.

6. Your own _____

_____

**Words To Consider**
*"Choose this day whom you will serve…*
*As for me and my house, we will serve the Lord."*
Joshua 24:15

# FORTY FOUR

# Life is for learning

You were born to live life to the fullest and to grow from each of your experiences. With each new situation you encounter, first ask yourself, "*What did I learn? Am I a wiser and more compassionate person because of what I experienced?*" Through your struggle to answer this question, you will slowly grow in knowledge and wisdom.

Often pain will be your greatest teacher. While comfort puts us to sleep (when things are going our way, we rarely ask "what am I learning from this situation?"), discomfort forces us to question our assumptions and consider new ways of looking at life.

Second, ask yourself, "*How much did I love?*" Those who have gone through the near-death experience report that at the moment of death, they focused on the love or lack of it in their lives. Material achievements, on the other hand, paled in significance. Nobody ever said at that critical moment, "I regret that I didn't spend more time at the office."

Thus, your most important teachings will involve matters of the heart. If life is for learning, all of your experiences can be reduced to a single lesson—the lesson of learning to LOVE.

## *Affirmations*

1. There is no such thing as a bad experience—I learn from everything that I encounter.

2. I rejoice that I am continually given the opportunity to grow in love.

3. Everything in my life brings me closer to God.

4. Onward and upward!

5. I am increasing in knowledge and wisdom each and every day.

6. Your own _____
_____

**Words To Consider**
*"Our greatest glory is not in never falling,*
*But in rising every time we fall."*
Confucius

# FORTY FIVE

# Faith

Faith is an attitude, a way of experiencing life. Faith arises when evidence is lacking. It is "the substance of things hoped for; the evidence of things unseen."

Nowhere is faith more necessary and more tested than in times of despair. No matter how much darkness you may feel, your faith can be kindled by remembering the metaphysical law—"What goes down must come up." Nothing lasts forever. With each new moment, anything becomes possible. As long as you have life, you have hope.

Through faith, those faced with insurmountable odds discover the inner strength to make it through. Glenn Cunningham overcame severe burns on his legs to become a world-class Olympic runner. Similar heroics occur every day among those who suffer traumatic injuries and life-threatening illnesses.

Faith indeed has the power to cure—physically, mentally, emotionally and spiritually. After healing a woman's illness, Christ told her, "Thy faith has made thee whole." Believing in getting well is a powerful force that can motivate your body and soul to strive for wholeness.

Over time, you will discover the evidence to back up your faith. As you step out in faith and the universe supports you, you can tell yourself, "I know that I will be provided for. It happened before, and it will happen again."

# Affirmations

1. My faith is making me whole.

2. I may see no solution, but God reveals the perfect answer.

3. I have a deep faith that new doors are opening before me.

4. I trust in what I cannot see.

5. I expect a miracle.

6. Your own _____

_____

**Words To Consider**
*"Faith is the bird that feels the light
and sings while the dawn is still dark."*
Proverb

# FORTY SIX

# My will and the Divine will are one

To understand the relationship between your personal will and your Higher will, think of yourself as a light bulb that carries 1 amp of current. When you tune in to your Higher will, you have access to not just one amp, but to ten, one hundred, one thousand amps—or any amount of current you want. Because you are tapping into the source of all light and power, your supply is unlimited—and so is the light you can radiate to others.

But letting go of the ego is not easy. We want to do things our way, in our own time, with our own requirements. We want to be in **control**. Yet in clinging to this limited frame of reference, we deny ourselves a much greater reality as well as an expanded potential for happiness, fulfillment and material abundance. This is why great souls have always affirmed, "Not my will, but Thy will be done."

You die to the ego so that you can be born to God. You die to the *part* so that you can be born to the *whole*. Ultimately, you can even overcome death itself. For when you learn to dwell in the higher mind, you will experience the part of yourself that never dies.

Go into meditation and listen for the whisperings of that universal source. Allow them to guide you and to show you the way in all of your affairs. Let the universe do its work **through** you. As you become a perfect channel for the Divine presence, you will affirm to that eternal part of yourself, "My will and the Divine will are one."

# Affirmations

1. I act in accordance with my Higher Self.

2. I am continually aligned with my higher purpose.

3. I do what God wants me to do.

4. When I contact the God-in-me, all things become possible.

5. I gladly die to my caterpillar self that I may be reborn as a butterfly.

6. Your own _____

_____

**Words To Consider**
*"The blossom vanishes of itself as the fruit grows.*
*So will your lower self vanish as the Divine grows within you."*
Vivekananda

# FORTY SEVEN

# Ask and you shall receive

"Ask and you shall receive. Seek and ye shall find. Knock and the door shall be opened. For everyone who asks receives, and he who seeks finds, and to him who knocks, it shall be opened."

You have no doubt heard these words and the wonderful promise they offer—that you are never given a wish without being given the power to make it come true. For the wish to be fulfilled, however, you must want it with all your heart.

There once was a seeker who asked a master teacher what he could do to achieve enlightenment. The master thought for a moment and then suddenly grabbed the seeker by his head and plunged it into a nearby rain barrel. The student struggled to get free but to no avail, until the teacher released him. As the half–drowned man emerged, gasping for oxygen, the teacher said, "When you want God as much as you just wanted that breath of air, then you will find the Infinite One."

Besides intensely desiring the good you seek, you must take active steps to make it happen. Pray as if everything depends upon God, but work as if everything depends upon you. Through this collaboration, you can successfully resolve any challenge you face.

Strive with all your heart and soul for the good you desire. If what you are seeking is for the highest good of all concerned, it will not be denied.

Ask and you shall receive. Seek and you shall find. Knock and the door shall be opened.

## *Affirmations*

1. I ask for what I want in life—and I receive it!

2. My prayers are always answered.

3. At every turn, opportunity appears before me.

4. I rejoice in my continuing good fortune.

5. Years of dedication and hard work have paid off. My ship is coming in.

6. Your own _____

_____

**Words To Consider**
*"Whatever you are ready for
is ready for you."*
Reverend Ike

# FORTY EIGHT

# Look to your source

There once was a woman who dreamed of opening a school for deaf children. "How can I possibly carry out this project?" she asked. "I have no money, no buildings, no employees, no one to turn to." To find a solution to her dilemma she turned inward and asked for guidance. Her still small voice replied, "What do you mean, no one to turn to? I am your SOURCE. Start forward in faith and allow me to guide you each step of the way. You will surely prosper, for with God, *all* things are possible." The woman followed her guidance and succeeded in raising the money for her school.

This story has been lived out thousands of times in human history. The seeds of great religions, businesses, educational institutions and artistic creations were sown by people who experienced direct communion with the **creative source** that resides in every human being.

Ask yourself, "What is the source of my happiness, health and prosperity? Is it my job, my spouse, my physician, or any other external mode?" While these outside avenues may be a means of reaching that source, they are not the source. That source is God–in–you.

Like a parent who wants the best for his children, your Father/Mother God is ready to bless you with all the good that you seek. Why not make direct contact with your source and drink from a fountain of plenty that will never run dry?

## *Affirmations*

1. I will look to God alone as my source.

2. God–in–me is my unlimited, overflowing supply of every kind of good.

3. When I look to my source, I am guided to make choices for my highest good.

4. Through my connection to Infinite Intelligence, all things are possible.

5. God–in–me provides for my every need.

6. Your own _____

_____

**Words To Consider**
*"Truth is within ourselves, it takes no rise*
*From outward things, whate'er you may believe.*
*There is an inmost center in us all,*
*Where truth abides in fullness."*
Robert Browning

# FORTY NINE

# Simplicity

Although we attempt to make it complex, the essence of life is simplicity. Being a good parent to your children, having a loving relationship with your partner, feeling needed by others—it is these fundamental requirements for love and appreciation that nurture the human spirit.

The theme of simplicity is repeated over and over in the great spiritual teachings. Jesus tells us that unless we become as little children, we cannot enter the kingdom of God. To receive the truth, we must make ourselves like a child—open, accepting and trusting. Too often, however, we get lost in the hectic pace of modern life and lose touch with our true priorities.

Look at your own life. Has it become overly complex? Have you found yourself burdened by too many possessions or responsibilities? Take a deep breath and ask yourself, "What steps can I take to reduce the clutter so that I may live simply and joyously?"

Think how little it takes to lift up your spirits—a smile from your child, an unexpected day of sunny weather, a cold drink on a hot afternoon. As you learn to simplify your life, you will experience a freedom of the soul and lightness of heart. These priceless gifts are yours when you learn to focus on what is truly essential.

## *Affirmations*

1.  It's a gift to be simple; it's a gift to be free.

2.  I focus on what is truly essential.

3.  I release all extra baggage from my life.

4.  I feel light and joyous.

5.  I take delight in the simplest of things; even the ordinary gives me pleasure.

6.  Your own _____

_____

**Words To Consider**
*"Our life is frittered away by detail ... Simplify, simplify."*
Thoreau

# FIFTY

# Protection

Protection is available to you at any time, in any place, if you  ask for it. When you reside in that God–consciousness in the center of your being, you can rise above any negativity that comes your way.

A priest was captured by a hostile government  and tortured for many months. Each time he faced his tormentors, he silently repeated the 23rd Psalm. By continually reciting this prayer during his captivity, he lifted himself into the Light and miraculously survived his ordeal.

Think back to those times in your life when you experienced this protection. Perhaps you narrowly escaped an accident, or emerged from a crisis that seemed to have no resolution. In each of these situations, give thanks for having been watched over and guided to safety.

The following Robe of Light invocation is used by many people to bring forth their inner protection. Recite it, or use your own favorite prayer when you feel the need for comfort or guidance.

### Robe of Light Prayer

*I clothe myself in a Robe of Light, composed of the Love and the Power and the Wisdom of God, not only for my own protection, but so that all who see it or come in contact with it may be drawn to God and be healed.*

*Use me, Mother/Father, to the utmost capacity for the coming of Thy kingdom on earth. Amen.*

# *Affirmations*

1. The light of God surrounds me; the love of God enfolds me; the power of God protects me; the presence of God watches over me. Wherever I am, God is.

2. My heart is not troubled nor am I afraid when I remember that God is with me.

3. I face the future confidently, knowing that I am protected.

4. The Lord is my shepherd. I shall not want.

5. I take refuge in my inner sanctuary. I am safe, secure, and serene.

6. Your own _____

_____

**Words To Consider**
*"Though I walk through the valley of the shadow of death,*
*I will fear no evil: for thou art with me;*
*Thy rod and thy staff they comfort me."*
The 23rd Psalm

# FIFTY ONE

# Character is destiny

Have you ever wondered about your future? The answer to your musings lies not in a crystal ball, but in your own character. Here is where your destiny is forged—you and no other are responsible for your life.

At times, your strength of character may be tested by trials and difficulties. In these instances, remember that *the best students are given the toughest problems*. A math teacher will assign his top calculus student a task that is worthy of his skill. Similarly, you possess the capabilities to successfully meet your present challenges.

Fortunately, you don't have to meet them alone; there is support to draw upon. If you make the effort to help yourself, the universe will meet you halfway. Your first step need not be one of action; perhaps you sincerely desire to make changes, but don't know how to start. Just ask for guidance, and the wheels of grace will be set in motion.

Character is destiny. It is the quality of your character that will determine your present happiness and future circumstances.

# *Affirmations*

1. I am the master of my fate. I am the captain of my soul.

2. I command success through every action. I am the success that I seek.

3. I know what I want out of life—and I get it.

4. I feel like a winner.

5. I let go of blaming others. I accept responsibility for my life.

6. Your own _____

_____

**Words To Consider**
*"What lies behind us and what lies before us,*
*are small matters when compared to what lies within us."*
Emerson

# FIFTY TWO

# Love your body

Perhaps the most beautiful tool you are given to work with is that of your physical body. The result of millions of years of evolution, your body is a divine temple that houses your spiritual self and expresses it in the physical world.

Your body is naturally intelligent. It knows how to repair itself and contains an innate wisdom that automatically carries on a whole host of functions without your conscious input. Your body will always communicate what it needs, if you just listen.

Coming from a tradition that denied the body, we often ignore its wisdom. But these are no longer the Middle Ages. We are living in a new era in which the body and soul are acknowledged as divine partners, working together for spiritual progress and evolution.

How have you been treating your body? Do you provide it with adequate amounts of food, water, exercise, fresh air and rest? When your body is sick, do you slow down, or do you become angry with it for interfering with your plans? When did you last give yourself a massage, or some other sensual pleasure?

Take a moment and express appreciation to your body for all that it has given you. Ask your body what it needs right now and then fulfill its request. You and your body are one. When you love and respect your body, you are loving and respecting yourself.

# *Affirmations*

1. I love my body just the way it is.

2. My body is the perfect size, shape and weight.

3. I give my body what it wants.

4. My body is healthy, strong, and radiant.

5. I treat my body like royalty.

6. Your own _____
_____

**Words To Consider**
*"If anything is sacred,
the human body is sacred."*
Walt Whitman

# Reflections on the Transformational Journey

*"And in the end, the love you take
is equal to the love you make."*
**The Beatles**

We are all on a journey—a journey of change and transformation. The journey is a movement toward wholeness, completeness, and union with the highest part of us. It is a journey of healing.

Over the years, I have learned a number of lessons about this journey which I have shared in *Words That Heal*.

**The journey takes time.** Change does not occur overnight, but rather in small, incremental, almost unnoticeable steps. As writer Jack Kerouac put it, "Walking on water wasn't built in a day." As you work with this material, be patient. Praise yourself for each small gain you make.

**The journey involves letting go of fear**, learning to trust yourself and others. Along with this process comes an opening of the heart to love and acceptance.

**The journey of transformation involves pain.** Alhough pain is often the neccessary stimulus that leads us to the path of change, this type of suffering actually *enhances* our existence. We grow **because** of our pain, not in spite of it.

**While you don't always get what you want,** you invariably get what you need for your maximum soul growth.

**Never give up.** Just when all seems hopeless, life can unexpectedly turn around. Never are you nearer the Light, than when the darkness is deepest.

**Help is available when you need it.** Ask with all your heart; your prayers will be answered.

**Each person is born into a unique set of circumstances** with challenges that are perfect for his or her growth and development. While Joan's important lessons lie in the area of work, Ann may be obsessed with relationships. One person's karma is another's grace.

**Everything that happens in your life occurs for your highest good.** There are no "bad" experiences, only opportunities to use each experience as a means to get closer to God.

In the end, we will all reach that state of wholeness and completeness. Once the inner reality shifts, the outer reality will follow. As you change your thoughts, you will change your world.

This is your challenge—to become a **co–creator** with the Infinite, and to learn to use its creative power wisely and lovingly. Claim your divine inheritance *now*. The universe can only say YES!

# Sample Affirmations

The following list of affirmations was chosen to assist you in applying affirmations to your daily life. The affirmations are formatted under seven distinct headings: Self–Esteem, Love and Relationships, Creative Self–Expression, Work/Vocation, Prosperity, Health, and Spiritual Development.

Use these categories to focus on your specific core issues. Thus, if work or career is of interest right now, turn to the Work/Vocation list of affirmations. You can work with the ones in the appendix, or create your own.

Many of these affirmations were selected from the main text. Allow yourself to be drawn to those that have the most significance for you. Once you have chosen your affirmations, you can apply the techniques from the affirmation chapter to work with them on an ongoing basis.

# Self–Esteem

I like myself.

I value myself.

I have something unique to offer.

I deserve to be happy.

I treat myself to the very best.

I am a good person.

I love myself just the way I am.

I accept myself as I am.

I feel good about me.

I like my essence.

I take responsibility for my well–being.

I take good care of myself.

I respect who I am.

I am confident and self-assured.

I am the master of my fate. I am the captain of my soul.

# Love and Relationships

As I feel self–love, I experience the love of others.

When I love others, others love themselves.

Love flows to and from me.

I radiate love to everyone I encounter.

I am lovable.

I am attracting open, loving relationships.

I am whole within myself. My partner is whole within
him/herself. Together we are one.

I feel good about being close.

I enjoy expressing my sexuality.

I am willing to risk myself in love.

I deserve love.

I draw to myself my ideal friends and lovers.

I am clear about what I want in a relationship.

I am ready for a relationship. I am ready for love.

I'd rather win love than arguments.

# Creative Self–Expression

Creative ideas are revealing themselves to me
each and every day.

I am excited about life. I have discovered my passion.

I am ready to release my inner barriers to fulfilling my
purpose on earth.

I am ready to go the whole way with my genius.

I am attuned to Divine inspiration.

Everything I need to know is revealed to me.

I am in constant communication with
my creative source.

I am changing and transforming
my old and limiting beliefs.

Through God-in-me, all things are possible.

Every moment in my life is infinitely creative.

I use my creative power to bring the best into my life.

I am the writer, director and actor of my own movie.

I trust myself. I trust my intuition.

# Work/Vocation

I am at the center of the Divine idea of my right and perfect
work for personal fulfillment, service to God
and financial abundance.

I am attracting the people, circumstances and finances to
make my dream come true.

By doing what I love, I make a comfortable living.

I am doing what I love and getting paid for it.

I have found the perfect career to support myself
in the world.

I am on the verge of a vocational breakthrough.

I am financially self–sufficient and happy in my work.

I offer a wonderful service for wonderful pay.

God is guiding me to fulfilling work.

I am always at the right place at the right time,
engaged in the right activity.

I am actualizing my full potential in the world.

My work is love in action.

I have a wonderful relationship with my co-workers
(or boss, employees, business partner, etc.).

Customers love our company and its products
(or services).

I feel great about what I do for a living.

# Prosperity

God–in–me is my unlimited, overflowing supply
of every kind of good.

I always have plenty of money.

A part of all I earn is mine to keep.

I invest wisely and responsibly.

The more I give, the more I am given to give.

My income exceeds my expenses.

I deserve to prosper.

My wealth contributes to my aliveness
and to the aliveness of others.

When I prosper, other people prosper.
When I succeed, other people succeed.

I have more than I need, and so I share with my world.

My cup runneth over.

There is more than enough to go around for everyone,
including me.

My personal connection to Universal Intelligence allows
large sums of money to flow to and through me.

God manifests through my life as abundance and prosperity
on all levels.

The more I win, the more others win.
The more others win, the more I win.
Therefore, I am winning more and more of the time.

I rejoice in my continuing good fortune.

# Health

God–in–me is my health right now.

God–in–me is my strength; I overflow with vitality.

Every day, in every way, I am getting better and better.

I love my body and treat it like royalty.

My body is the perfect size and shape.

I am a powerful person.

All the cells of my body are daily bathed in the perfection of my divine being.

I am healthy, happy and radiant.

I radiate good health.

My body is a safe and pleasurable place for me to be.

My sleep is relaxed and refreshing.

I have all the energy I need to accomplish my goals and to fulfill my desires.

God's love heals me and makes me whole.

My body is healed, restored and filled with energy.

# Spiritual Development

The Divine breath flows through me and blesses me.

I am a channel for love and healing.

I affirm Divine order, and all parts of my life fall into place.

Everything I need comes to me.

All is well in my life; I am truly blessed.

All things are working together for good in my life.

The universe nurtures and protects me at all times
and in all places.

God is with me through every change—guiding, protecting
and directing me all the way.

I dwell in the presence of God's eternal love.

The Lord is my shepherd.

All that my heart desires will come to pass.

When one door closes, another door opens.
Whenever I seem to lose something of value,
it is only to make room for something better.

I am divinely guided.

Focusing on the present heals my fear of the unknown.

I expect a miracle.

When I put my spiritual development first,
all of my other needs are fulfilled.

Higher wisdom expresses itself daily
in all aspects of my life.

I am worthy to receive the unlimited offerings
of the universe.

I see all problems as disguised opportunities.

I listen to myself and confidently act upon what I hear.

I affirm only the best for myself and others.

God's wisdom illumines me, casting light on my path.

When I follow my heart, the universe supports me.

I let go and let God.

My persistence and determination work miracles.

It's all unfolding perfectly.

Life has great things in store for me.

I give thanks and praise for all things.

I welcome change into my life.

I learn from every situation I encounter.

I let go of the old and make way for the new.

I forgive myself and others. I am free.

Forgiveness is its own reward.

I bless and release all those who have caused me pain.

As I forgive, so am I forgiven.

Everywhere I look, I see opportunities to serve.

My will and the Divine will are one.

I am continually aligned with my higher purpose.

At every turn, good fortune appears before me.

My faith is making me whole.

Every experience in life brings me closer to God.

# About the Author

Douglas Bloch is an author, teacher and counselor residing in Portland, Oregon. *Words That Heal* grew out his own spiritual quest and is the first of a series of books on spiritual healing that he plans to author. Mr. Bloch is available for lectures and seminars on affirmations and other aspects of self-healing. If you would like to contact him, you may do so at 4226 NE 23rd Avenue, Portland, OR. 97211.